SIGNIFYING RAPPERS

SIGNIFYING RAPPERS

DAVID FOSTER WALLACE

AND

MARK COSTELLO

BACK BAY BOOKS

Little, Brown and Company

New York Boston London

Back Bay Books / Little, Brown and Company
Hachette Book Group
237 Park Avenue, New York, NY 10021
littlebrown.com

Originally published in paperback by Ecco Press, November 1990
First Back Bay paperback edition, July 2013

Back Bay Books is an imprint of Little, Brown and Company, a division of Hachette
Book Group, Inc. The Back Bay Books name and logo are trademarks of Hachette
Book Group, Inc.

Permissions acknowledgments appear on page 152.

The publisher is not responsible for websites (or their content) that are not owned by
the publisher.

The Hachette Speakers Bureau provides a wide range of authors for speaking
events. To find out more, go to hachettespeakersbureau.com or call (866) 376-6591.

ISBN 978-0-316-22583-0
Library of Congress Control Number 2013940549

10 9 8 7 6 5 4 3 2 1

RRD-C

Printed in the United States of America

PREFACE

MARK COSTELLO

IN EARLY 1989, I received a call from David Wallace, my closest friend and former college roommate, who was living at his parents' home in Illinois. His news was that he would be returning to grad school in aesthetics at Harvard in the fall, commencing a long slog toward a doctorate and an imagined career as a philosophy don at some leafy, sleepy campus. As I was already in the Boston area (I am a native of the place), he suggested that we live together one more time.

By April 1989, Dave and I were established in a second-floor apartment with two bedrooms, a sitting room, and a kitchen (which we cooked in maybe twice), all for six hundred bucks a month. The apartment was on Houghton Street, on the border of Somerville and ethnic Northeast Cambridge, a place of inward-sagging tenements, clapboard siding, and deep porches, Boston's trademark tripledeckas. Wires crossed the alleys, telephone and laundry lines. Yards were small, cement, and well defended by bulldogs and Madonnas.

Dave had arrived, as always, with a broken box spilling books. In college, we had cowritten a fair amount of comedy. But the soup stock of our friendship had always been coreading, passing paperbacks around like mashed potatoes at a family dinner. Nathanael

West's *The Day of the Locust,* published with *Miss Lonelyhearts,* was the first book Dave unpacked, day one, before he even got his towels arranged the way he liked them. Then *Slouching Towards Bethlehem,* Joan Didion's '60s journalism, with its flavors of Yeats and *The Bacchae.* Vollmann's *Rainbow Stories* was another fave — not stories but reportage and, given its milieu (drunk tanks, sex shops, prostitutes), not much of a rainbow either. But the central chunk of reading was a group of skitter-smart cultural critics: Todd Gitlin on TV, Greil Marcus on Elvis and "race" music, and the king of the apartment, Lester Bangs.

Signifying Rappers is dedicated to an *L. Bangs,* which sounds like one of Oswald's Dallas pseudonyms but is in fact none other than Leslie Conway "Lester" Bangs, born in 1948 in Escondido, California, to Woody Guthrie's people, Dust Bowlers blown west. Raised by an unnervingly religious mother, Bangs began to churn out antic and articulate bulletins on surfer music and early California grunge while still in high school. A *Rolling Stone* man by the age of twenty-one, he was fired after a few short years for all-around rebellion. Bangs was dead by thirty-four of a drug overdose. His cantankerous rock writing appeared in a weighty collection, *Psychotic Reactions and Carburetor Dung* (edited by his good friend Greil Marcus), in 1988, just in time to blow our minds.

Psychotic Reactions is assembled from Bangs's weekly album reviews, concert coverage, liner notes, and long essays about funk, punk, metal, and New Wave published in *Rolling Stone, Creem,* and the *Village Voice.* Like an angry jungle idol (an angry music critic? an angry *record reviewer?*), Bangs seemed to be demanding *something* from the villagers: dispute, concurrence, outrage, virgin sacrifice. He was everything that young men could glom on to. A bit of a Belushi, he was charismatically fat, unkempt, mutton chopped, with the coolest

Fu Manchu around. His best prose, when he took the time to write it, evoked the young Saul Bellow—earthy, slangy, yet in its rhythms stately. Think Charles Lamb with a dose of Bugs and Groucho and quite possibly the clap. Dave, like most writers, lived in a resentful semi-fear of the six or seven influential book reviewers in the land, and he loved the way Bangs salted his reviews with rants against the notion of reviewers as priests of group taste. If I, LB, bright-eyed fat man, say that an album is good, real, true, authentic, the essence of the zeitgeist now, compelling you and all your lemming-friends to run right out and buy it, isn't this whole loop-de-loop of manufactured zeitgeist kind of, you know, *weird?* Empty? Shallow? Sad? Bangs took it further, noting that even these ironies had their own ironies. Rebelling against the commercializing ballyhoo of reviewery, he was upping his own stature as a critic. The more he says don't listen, the more we do exactly that. Yet Bangs was never cynical. Maturing from his first niche as a bumptious enthusiast into a sort of heartsick and satiric Molière, Bangs never lost his faith in pop's capacity to move us toward connection with one another.

Funny thing. Bangs wrote his best prose when dissatisfied. When he came upon a group he truly loved, the Lambian sentences foundered. He needed them no more. He sent the Maker thank-you notes for the music he loved. Blunt. In grunts and oinks and growls. His message in those oinks was this: IT'S GOOD TO BE ALIVE.

&

When I agreed to live with Dave, he did not warn me that a few months earlier, in October 1988, he had attempted suicide with pills. He kept this fact from me for reasons of his own. Twice in college, we had been through Dave's breakdowns and defeated journeys back to Illinois. He could not abide kindness or niceness. A good midwestern kid, he understood politeness. Love was the other engulfing extreme. But in between the two, on mankind's wide radio dial, were two shitty AM stations known as the Nice and the Kind, which seemed to play a lot of ads and bands like Mr. Mister. Dave kept the suicide attempt from me in part because he wanted to have fun goddamnit, *fun*, and because he dreaded the tepidities of kindness.

Lester Bangs spoke directly to, directly at, depression. He made the case for life as judging, watching, loving, and joining—hearing as adhering. Bangs was loyal in defense of acts he cared for. He wove a case for caring out of cloth that was attractive and accessible to Dave: the music in the record stores and on the radio. We should pursue our pop epiphanies and be wide open to them. Bangs urged his readers to stop reading and get out to clubs and rocking hell-holes, which blessedly abounded on both banks of the Charles. Dave was more of a bar man than a club man, but with Saint Lester's assistance I could often talk him into a musical crawl through the town. In 1989, humanity lacked the great and hungry search tools of today, Google, Yahoo, YouTube, Bing. But on mild Friday nights in dense-packed urban areas, we did possess another life-enlarging search engine. It was called walking. We were two blocks from the I-Square Men's Bar, basically a veterans' hall converted in the '70s to Boston's home o' punk. Western Front on Western Ave was the finest ska and reggae venue north of NYC, where dreadlocked pos-semen and white kids in hemp ponchos bonded in a spleef fog over Burning Spear's latest album. There was Green Street for Chicago blues and Cantab Lounge for R&B, a glorious Stax reenactment where beehived women who had once been members of the Vandellas would tear the living shit out of "I've Been Loving You Too Long" on a tiny and somehow naked-making stage. Plough & Stars had Irish trad, beatnicky poetry, white guys playing contrapuntal Robert Johnson on steel-bodied guitars.

Inbound on Mass Ave was a basement place called Wally's Café, with jazz all night and funk on Sunday. Wally's was the snuggest of these venues, yet Miles Davis had played it in the '50s at a time when BU seminary student Martin Luther King lived on the block and occasionally wandered in. Also on Mass Ave was Dave's favorite destination, the Middle East Café, which had started as a budget kebab house for scruffy undergrads, expanding through a back wall into the next building, where the owner built a grotto for belly dancing shows. Belly dancing segued with complete illogic into stand-up comedy, trance and dance, performance art, electronica. Friday night felt infinite in such a place. A long walk around Cambridge might bring every kind of groove to you, along with and above the other city sounds, the hissing of the buses and the imprecating bums.

Things went along like this, improvised, unbalanced, until one particular weekend still in spring when a friend of mine, a lefty lawyer for the tugboat workers' union, came to crash at Houghton Street, unpacking with his toothbrush two mix tapes. Slick Rick. Schoolly D. Ice T. Chuck D. This was rap. Annoyingly, my friend seemed to know more about rap at large and our own oddball Boston scene in particular than we did. Did we know, for example, that most white-owned clubs, fearful of the "element" rap might attract, refused to book it to their stages? For this reason, the most "prestigious" hip-hop venue in the city was a dismal former roller derby circuit from the 1930s bearing the alluring name of Chez Voo Disco Rink. Roller Derby, murdered French, disco anything—the potential of this weirdness was quite clear. Dave had by then already maniacally transcribed the subversive wordplay of two cuts by Schoolly D, pen in hand, big silver boom box to his ear.

&

Signifying Rappers was shaped by several valences. The first was rap's successful crossover in the form of Tone Lōc's "Wild Thing," which peaked at number two on *Billboard*'s Hot 100 chart in 1988, and "Funky Cold Medina," which sold two million copies as we wrote these essays sewn together as a book. Boston's own Bobby Brown, a son of Roxbury's Orchard Park projects, had a number two pop-charted hit with "My Prerogative," which is or isn't really rap, though Brown was thought to be a rapper. Bobby Brown's success *hit home* in Boston's clubland. People knew him, had known him, or imagined they had known him. Kids *like* Bobby Brown were dime-a-dozen. Like Liverpudlian rockers after the Beatles made it big, these aspiring young rappers and promoters shared a dizzy sense of possibility.

The second trend in Boston, more my concern than Dave's, was an eruption of gun violence that dominated the old *Boston Globe*'s conscientious headlines. The summer of 1989 was the bloodiest in Boston's history and nobody seemed to know why. This wasn't Crip-on-Blood, the clash of corporatized gang brands. This was closer to slaying as folk art, Boston being topographically a city of coves and necks, peninsulas and squares, an archipelago of many little inter-hostile 'hoods. The shootings by black teens (often on bicycles, a haunting touch — the pedal-by killing) were written up as symptoms of imploding opportunity, atrocious public schools, a sky-high dropout rate, all of which was taken, in some vague way, as an indictment of forced busing in Boston, court-ordered in 1974 and still in force in 1989. Busing was the grand reform, experiment, and sucking civic chest wound of my Massachusetts childhood. In 1989, Year 13 of the experiment, violence seemed to menace the whole vision of the City Beautiful and certainly the City Unified. Pro-busing liberals said, well what did you expect? Kids in Orchard Park have *no other way out*. Then as if on cue came million-selling Bobby Brown to light the unreal path out of Orchard Park and poverty, and somehow deal the liberals another blow. This was the municipal neurosis of the summer.

Meanwhile, back on Houghton Street, Dave and I plied our jaunty and disreputable bachelor lifestyle. I would come home from the office in the evenings, finding Dave emerging from the day's fifth shower or sitting in his favored velour easy chair, legs crossed in his dainty way, a cheap Mead notebook in his lap, a Winston Gold 100, those extra-long smokes of the trailer parks, burning in his slender fist. He considered himself on hiatus. This, he proclaimed, was Vacationing Dave. He had come through gory legal edits on his great story collection *Girl with Curious Hair;* it would be published in August. Harvard would start in September.

But Vacationing Dave was always working. He had come to Cambridge in April fired up to write a long essay on the making and the watching of pornographic movies. This project grew and swallowed others. Often I would come home and find him with his notebook, trying to decode the awful yet addictive anti-fantasy of porn. The work, commenced in hope and inspiration, had become a maze of paradox or simple contradiction, the gnashing, the effable, the gross. Porn's stupendous dumbness (hokey sets, bad dialogue) was a central attribute. But how to write smartly of the many functionings of Dumb? How to write with dignity and distance of store-bought arousal? His answer, when inspiration faltered, was often to chart and stack the paradoxes, creating ever more elaborated mazes. This was writing as compulsion, not as pleasure. He left his chair and notebook to escape to Cambridge clubland with a growing sense of stalemate.

In June, as I recall, Dave went to Manhattan for a dreaded authors' panel. A fellow panelist launched a rote attack on rap as violent, anti-white, anti-women, bling-obsessed. Dave defended the artists he knew, praising the dexterity, the wordplay, the raucous, raw assault on the sententious Babbittry of the Age of Reagan. He loved the easy postmodernity, songs built out of pieces of other songs, rappers rapping that their rap was better than another rapper's rap, which had itself attacked some *other* rapper's rap. Songs about nothing that burst nonetheless with appetite and personality.

Lee Smith, an editor in New York, intrigued by Dave's defense of the form, suggested that he write an essay that might have carried the title "How Rap, Which You Hate, Is Not What You Think, and Is Interesting as Hell, and, If Offensive, a Useful Sort of Offensive Given What Is Happening Today." The posture was all Bangs, of course, and it felt good. Plus he could transport some of the themes and maybe some of the pages from the porn book as well. (The discussion of Synecdoche in Section 1B strikes me as an import.) Always upbeat in beginning, glad to have an excuse to put the stalled porn project aside, Dave quickly and happily drafted or grafted the first three "D." sections of *Signifying Rappers* in June and early July 1989. These sections are twitchy and tetchy, fence as much as sentence. They are also optimistic (with hedges and cavils), openhearted, extroverted. Rap, he tells the reader, has a messy forest history. It is developing, organic, young. Yet it possesses true fart-at-the-party protest potential. Section 1B explores the history and terms, the points of "incongruity," especially the three-way influence (later the source of so much unease in *Infinite Jest*) between the artist, the consumer, and the medial technology that links and separates them.

"Our point of departure, essay-wise," states Dave in 1B, "was always less what we knew than what we felt, listening; less what we liked than why." This picture of critical impetus is fissured down its face, of course, saying that we care less for *knowing* than for *feeling*. At the same time, though, we need to know *why* we feel a certain thing, or any thing at all, in response to Schoolly D. Celebrating feeling is a good Bangsian oink. But the nervous asker, why and why and why and why, is self-inspecting Dave failing to escape the planetary orbit of his doubts. I like the early sections of the "D." side of the essay for this very ceaseless back-and-forth. There are entire handsome paragraphs constructed end to end of sentences that contradict themselves in subtle ways. The reader's pupils, moving left to right along each line of type two decades later, seem to pace the floor alongside a worried, yearning, baffled, battling David Wallace.

Yearning was the yeast of DFW, life in crudest form, and yet it makes the baking rise. Yearning haunts the fiction, brothers seeking sisters, genius isolados who seek the ordinary things of friendship: trust, concern, affection, talk. Throughout the early "D." sections of *Signifying Rappers*, you can hear the hope and humor too. There's a bounce in the prose that captures some of the fun, goddamnit fun, to be found around Boston that summer.

On weekends, we would rise at a gentleman's hour and stumble to S&S deli in Inman for bacon and eggs, which we ate while sharing the papers, the *Globe* with its brooding on Roxbury shootings and the *Phoenix*, the city's much-beloved alternative tabloid, fusing the best and hippest music reviews with encyclopedic club listings, all of it bound together by fine-print personals (*man seeks man for spanking*, etc.) and page upon page of sex ads. In the afternoons, we played pickup basketball with Italian kids in muscle shirts at Saint Anthony of Padua's. (Dave, spazzy off the tennis court but—make no mistake—intensely competitive everywhere, chipped my tooth on a rebound.) Later, we would stroll to Central Square to comb the discount bins at Cheapo, the shabby and eclectic record store across the street from Cantab and the Middle East Café. The clerks at Cheapo were a sort of floor show of their own, smirking at your putrid musical tastes while leading you toward manna. Ask them for an album by Ken Maynard (1920s singing cowboy, girlish, lonesome, minimal, Cormac McCarthy in song) and the clerks would: (a) scoff at Cowboy Ken and (b) name his whole discography and ask which song you wanted. Cheapo clerks were into William Shatner as a singer and Charles Manson, that chanteuse, long before the mainstream ironists at Rhino Records laid claim to them. They tolerated everything, all tastes and customer requests, except what was then called "hard" rap—the harsh and the defiant—which the Cheapo clerks believed to be essentially unmusical. A store that had entire bins for Aboriginal didgeridoo and Wendy / Walter Carlos's sex-changed / switched-on Bach had only a few rap albums, which the clerks seemed reluctant to sell, to know, even to touch.

At four or five, our friends would start to call us or we them. Evening plans were laid with the care of an invasion. If I told you I was going to the Middle East at ten to catch a rap revue, you met me there or missed me altogether. Plans with friends had weight and stakes in those pre-texting days because they were uncorrectable once the night got rolling.

Rap night at the Middle East was a raffish, gaudy mess, emceed on that Ali Baba stage by a hustler in a tracksuit, the same kid every

week. The tone at the club on other nights was arch, smart, poisonous, like Brecht at a Weimar cabaret. Weirdo acts were ushered on
and off, freakish, winking, avant-garde, midgets in tuxedos playing
Velvet Underground. The rappers revolted against this. With their
dental grilles and dollar-sign necklaces, their carefully drilled but
totally stolen dance moves, they were closer to Liberace than to
Black Liberation. They wanted to do something strange for Cambridge: entertain. But different heartfelt aspects of these extrava-
ganzas seemed to crash against one another, the wraparound
shades like African dictators, the stiff-backed postures of the Nation
of Islam, the relentless (and yet clowning) grabbing at the crotch to
evoke gunselism and gangbanging, a fraught topic in that bloody
summer. Plus it was all too loud on a shitty sound system, an assault
that left us deaf and shaking on the long walk home through sleeping, dumpy neighborhoods. Dave's question on those walks was
always the essential one: "So — did that show *suck?* Or was it kind
of crazy, great, and free?"

In the morning I would leave for work and Dave would go to
his notebooks to rehash the night's impressions and dilemmas.
After he wrote these lively if conflicted sections (1B and 1C are
examples), the mazes rose again for him. The prose stopped flow-
ing. He asked me to read what he had written. At night, we would
walk or take a drive and talk it over.

Driving was a major social easer for Dave Wallace. Normal
conversational requirements — listening while thinking, while watching face- and body-language, while processing these sometimes
undermining messages (your voice says that you're interested, your
face says that you're bored), while *also* wondering about one's own
mixed messages of interest, boredom, politeness, contempt — could
be a burden. Talking was easier when driving because both parties,

seated, safety-belted, were positioned to stare out at the same relax-
ing blankness of the highway. The highway, saving eye contact,
made interaction bearable when Dave's nerves began to fray. His
mood improved on drives at two AM with girlfriends to the beaches
north of Boston or west to Walden Pond, an oasis in the suburbs
now, where we would go swimming in the deep and spring-fed
pond. Walden's water tastes the way a sidewalk smells just before it
rains. The water is *very* hard and excellent for swimming, like velvet
drawn across the skin. Dave would roll his tan corduroys up and
wade like Alfred Prufrock and worry, just a little, about snapping
turtles. But he was happy; you could hear it. He felt good.

On occasions when we did not overlap in the apartment or take
a drive together, I sometimes wrote my reply to parts of his rap
essay. A yeah-but or a what-if, left on his desk. It was Dave's idea to
incorporate my responses and turn the essay into a coauthored
book with intercut voices. The structure (three chapters aping the
Hegelian thesis, anti-, synthesis) was a Dave idea, implemented
through his funny, fussy letter-numbered subsections, 1A, 2B, 3C,
2D, 3F, 3H, which give the book a tense and teeming ambience,
appropriately urban, like a mad apartment tower full of pissed-off,
squabbling paragraphs who all want war with the landlord.

I wrote two sections in late summer. One passage was in Dave's
mode—internalized, discursive, the drama of the head. Subtly,
our dance positions shifted. Summer waned and he was feeling
sicker—more anxious, less directed, less able to sluice his thoughts
in a productive or even non-scary direction. Harvard neared,
depression loomed. By the time he wrote section 3H of the book—
a sermon, really; lucid, brave, abrasive—he had swung around to
the belief that rap was not the much-needed f-u to Reaganite
America but rather a Trojan horse of heart and cerebellum, a "pro-

test" so beset with muddy motives and hypocrisy that it could not help but fail. It was made to fail, born to be co-opted and subsumed into the junky ferrywake of media's caching.

Isolation, solipsism, the dying of connection — these were the great enemies of Bangs. As summer passed at Houghton Street, the chill of isolation spread. I remember fewer visitors, less passionate, dorm-style discussion, fewer nights of roaming, and then none at all. School started in September. Dave, who had once "done" philosophy with savantish ease, and who had moreover planned to make a professorial living by this gift, found in 1989 that he had lost the knack of college. He struggled to listen to lectures, squirmed while reading syllogistic arguments for Beauty. He drank more, and alone. These pages, both as writing and as voice-and-thought collage, are the last work he would finish before walking into Harvard student health services one cold autumn afternoon and politely disclosing dogged thoughts of suicide.

Part of my response to the darker turn at Houghton Street can be glimpsed in two overtly journalistic sections that Dave placed at the start and the end of the book. Section 1A narrates an afternoon in a raggedy rap studio in Roxbury midway through the murder wave, the jaded young producers and plump teenage wannabes, everybody stardusted by Bobby Brown's example. The coda (section 3I) is a brief account of a Peace Rally, an anti-gang event and free city-sponsored rap concert held on a hot day in August at Roxbury Community College. The concert was supposed to bring the rival groups from Orchard Park and Franklin Park and Melnea Cass together for a giant hatchet burying. Victims of shootings, mothers without sons, teenagers in wheelchairs, ministers, and politicians would urge the kids through crackly PAs to "Just have fun!" and "Quit the bangin', y'all!" The hottest local rappers would be there. Gang Starr was the big act, rolling stage-ward though the crowd in a white prom-rental limousine, a humorously humble stab at glitz. The rumor was that Bobby Brown himself would magically appear to rap us back to unity again. Just in case Bobby for some reason couldn't make it, there was also a huge and highly Irish police presence, barricades and helicopters, paddy wagons, a line of panting German shepherd dogs. These journalistic sections are a Didionish visit, homage to her travelogues through '60s California, people trapped inside the colorful soap bubbles called their personalities, rising on vast updrafts of the culture until they pop.

Throughout this book I'm saying tut-tut to my coauthor. Rap is sterile, closed, and circular if you understand it only as something on your tape deck, in your head. But it's also here and now, a city and a summer. Actual people, foolish, astute, venal, and dreaming, are writing the rhymes and mixing the tapes. They're passing through those Gaelic barricades for peace. It's cheating to avoid this life and call the whole thing lifeless. And it's tragic to conclude, from this supposed lifelessness, that you have nothing left to say. The tut-tut is me begging: come on, brother, just get off the couch and let's go *out*.

A note on the new edition: *Signifying Rappers* was originally published in May of 1990 with a short discography and a full transcription of the sampled and lyrical overlays of the classic hip-hop single "Paid in Full" by Eric B. & Rakim. In an effort to declutter things, these appendices have been cut to focus on the main text of the book.

This main text, along with the original acknowledgments, has been left for the most part as-is, or as-was. The book is a deeply dorked-out artifact of 1989, bristling with quick and cryptic references to Howard Beach, Dick Gephardt, the Tawana Brawley kidnapping, the TV shows and ad campaigns of that post-Reagan hangover. (Today the shorthand might be Newtown, nip slips, Dancing Baby, and Wayne LaPierre.) Does anyone remember Arsenio Hall or the California Raisins? Will these references fall flat for readers under forty?

It's a question and a problem. *Signifying Rappers* shoots for (and shoots *at*) the large abiding themes of corporatized mass culture, a particular kind of merchandized outrage that haunts and dominates the nation still. Perversely, though, while taking the "eternal" view, these sentences insistently date themselves to 1989, using words like *new, soon, lately, this year, now*. Terms like these don't age well. They introduce time's particular fragility to things, like the sell-by date on a milk carton. And this, ironically, is an abiding warning of the book, the furnace of all fads, the trash of temporality. But as time-bound—'89-bound—as these pages may seem at first, in rereading I'm struck by the poise and timelessness of particular passages of my coauthor's prose:

> Like the drum machines and scratch, sample and backbeat, the rapper's "song" is essentially an upper layer in the dense weave of *rhythm* that, in rap, usurps melody and harmony's essential functions of identification, call, counterpoint, movement, and progression, the play of woven noises...dance beats that afford unlimited bodily possibility, married rhythmically to complexly stressed lyrics that assert, both in message and meter, that things can never be other than what *IS*.

Well, wow. Rap is poetry. It is made of beat and meter — that is, marching time. I'm not sure what to make of the complex interplay of time, text, tension, and temporality in this little book, but it's probably best to leave it for the reader largely undisturbed.

July 2013

for l. bangs

1. ENTITLEMENT

M.

(1A)

The schools in a portion of Boston stretching from just south of South Boston through Roxbury and into Dorchester are districted with a similar effect: the predominantly black areas are cut away from the predominantly white areas.

—Morgan v. Hennigan, *U.S. District Court for Massachusetts, 1974*

THE SEEK BUTTON on the Ford's radio is working. The downtown recedes. Miles of neighborhoods fill the windshield. The SEEK function locks on someplace in stereo, college FM probably. 'Yeah,' a new friend says. 'Whas up. Whas goin on.' The radio has another button, VOL↑, which gets jacked repeatedly while the Ford hurtles, happily, to the source of the noise. Not to the station's broadcast booth on a campus across the river, nor to its transmission towers in the suburbs, but rather to RJam Productions in North Dorchester, where black kids from Boston's now integrated high schools—Latin, Madison Park, Jeremiah Burke, Mattapan—cut demos and dream of being bigger than even the radio's new friend, a young man named Schoolly D who right now, at speaker-damaging volume, sounds darn big. 'Before we start this next record...,' Schoolly's saying. The record in question's called "Signifying Rapper," a brief, bloody tale of ghetto retribution from Side 2 of Schoolly's *Smoke Some Kill.* The cut's intro, spoken into echo-chamber emptiness over stolen Led Zep licks, remains, even as bleeped for airplay, the deepest 30 seconds of rap yet: 'Yeah,' Schoolly says

Whas up
Whas goin on
Before we start this next record
I gotta put my shades on
So I can feel cool
Remember that law?
When you had to put your shades on to feel cool?
Well it's still a law
Gotta put your shades on
So you can feel cool
I'm gonna put my shades on
So I can't see
What you aint doin
And you aint doin nothin
You aint doin nothin
That I [unintelligible]
Well let's get on with this [bleep] anyway:

Maybe the radio has blundered like Coronado into a full-blown Schoolly D Retrospective, covering both years of his career, including all 14 selections from *Smoke Some Kill.* If so, we'll soon be hearing another classic, Schoolly's "Black Man," which samples a tape of Black Panther 'Minister of Justice' H. Rap Brown declaring: *You can't do your own thing if your own thing aint the right thing.* The brain's SEEK function locks on a memory of hearing a tape of Robert Kennedy plead for peace in some torn-up ghetto, saying: *Reject the Bull Connors and the Rap Browns, the racial extremists of either color;* and we're now on the John F. Fitzgerald Expressway, named after RFK's populist mayor grandfather, the Honorable John F. Fitzgerald, himself a kind of H. Blarney Brown back when the Irish were bottom dogs in Boston. So we're listening to an '80s admirer of a '60s protest populist once attacked as a demagogue by the grandson of the demagogue on whose namesake we ride.

The black areas are cut away from the white areas, a federal judge ruled in '74, and evidence is everywhere that nothing's changed since then. On the southbound left of the Fitzgerald Expressway pass 20 blocks of grim Irish Catholic housing projects, the westernmost border of Belfast, complete with Sinn Féin graffiti and murals depicting a glorious United Ireland, a neighborhood where the gadfly will get his fibula busted for praising the '74 court order that bused 'Them' from wherever it is 'They' live — *the Third World fer chrissakes* — into 97% white South Boston. On the expressway's right is the place the fibula-busters are talking about: the simultaneous northern border of Haiti, Jamaica, and Georgia; a territory maps of Boston call North Dorchester.

Uniting the two sides of the expressway is just about nothing. Both neighborhoods are tough and poor. Both hate the college world across the river, which, because of Boston's rotten public schools, they will never enter as freshmen. And kids from both neighborhoods can do this hating to the beat of undergraduate radio, which this fine morning features suburban kids with student debt broadcasting the art of a ghetto Philadelphian roughly their age, once much poorer than they but now, on royalties from *Smoke Some Kill,* very much richer.

Not that the shared digging of black street music is news, or even new: 20 years ago, when *Morgan v. Hennigan,* Boston's own

Brown v. Board of Education, was inching through the courts, and even dark-complected Italians were sometimes unwelcome in the Irish precincts east of the expressway, kids in Boston's Little Belfast sang along with James Brown over the radio

> *Say it loud*
> *I'm black and I'm proud*
> *Say it loud*
> *I'm black and I'm proud!*

Except that halfway through the infectious funk, the crewcuts realize what they're saying: Jesus Christ, 'I'm proud to be *black*' fer chrissakes, like when you're in the porno store, you know, and you get lost or something and you find yourself in the *men's* part, you know? not the part *for* men the part *about* men, Jesus, and you get the hell outta there. And so they hum/mumble the suppressed parts

> *Say it loud*
> *I'm mmm hum proud*
> *Say it loud*
> *Mum hum hum proud!*

And those mumbling white funk fans from '68 were the nephews of Little Richard lovers, and the sons of soldiers who whipped Hitler to a Duke Ellington–influenced soundtrack.

But rap isn't funk, rock, or jazz, and the vast crossover move, broadcasting 'ghetto' music over college radios to ghettos of a different color, is no simple re-enactment of past crossovers. How, for example, does the sing-along fan of *Smoke Some Kill* mumble his way through these lines

Black is beautiful
Brown is [sick? slick? stiff?]
Yellow's OK
But white aint shit.

℥

RJam Productions, modestly headquartered in a mixed black/Hispanic Fields Corner section of North Dorchester, is as follows:

- One (1) four-car garage fitted with dubbing and remastering gear worth more than most of the rest of the real estate on the block;
- One (1) Touchtone telephone (leased);
- Two (2) Chevy Blazers, vanity-plated RJAM1 and RJAM2, each equipped with cellular phones and slick tape decks (also leased);
- One (1) VCR with Kathleen Turner's *Body Heat* cued up on the morning in question;
- Most important, eight (8) promising acts under binding contract.

If—as has happened to many local labels—RJam were liquidated to satisfy creditors, these would be the pieces. But there are stores of value in the converted garage beyond the reach of the auctioneer's gavel. Schoolly D, the original Signifying Rapper, looms irresistibly from the pages of rap fanzines *Hip-Hop* and *The Source;* and RJam's prime, unauctionable asset is the consuming ambition of the artists in its stable to be the next Schoolly D. Or the next Ice T or Kool Moe Dee or L.L. Cool J, or whoever's the special hero of the kid

7

cutting the demo. On this particular morning, the dream is to be the next MC Lyte—a hard-rapping woman known for jams like "Lyte Vs. Vanna Whyte" and "10% Dis"—since today is Tam-Tam's day, and Tam-Tam is, at 16, a tough girl in the MC Lyte mold who, like MC Lyte, can dance, look good, and tell men to beat it, all at once.

Or so claims Tam-Tam's producer, promoter, and Dutch uncle, Gary Smith, who opened RJam on Martin Luther King's birthday, 1989, with his older brother Nate. Nate, the elder statesman, is 25. Gary, 22, runs the company while Nate travels with his boyhood-friend-turned-boss, quadruple-platinum, Prince-derived rapper/singer Bobby Brown. RJam was founded in part with an investment from the 23-year-old multimillionaire Brown, a native of Roxbury. Brown now lives in Los Angeles.

Nate and Gary Smith turn a healthy profit making demos at $500/tape, but the brothers aren't in the health business. Their aim: to follow in the corporate footsteps of Rush Productions, a once similarly tiny production company run from a basement in Hollis, Queens, that has, since its basement days, given America the Def Jam label, Public Enemy, L.L. Cool J, the Beastie Boys, and much of the rest of that culture-quake called rap. Gary Smith doesn't compare RJam to Def Jam; but, like Rush / Def Jam's Russell Simmons, Gary produces pop, soul, and R&B as well as straight rap, and actually prefers R&B. But how many sophomores at nearby Jeremiah Burke can afford to dream in R&B, to front music lessons and $500 for an nth-hand sound setup, find three friends to learn drums, bass, and keyboards, and then raise another $500 to make a demo at RJam? Anybody with a larynx can rap, however, and RJam's brisk business in rap demos pays the taxman, Boston Edison, and the Chevrolet Motor Credit Corp.

Twenty minutes farther south on the Fitzgerald Expressway,

across the Neponset River and into the pricey suburbs, is the scene of John Cheever's boyhood, more recently celebrated as Massachusetts Miracle country, where technology ventures are started at the rate of five per week, four of which will fail within 12 months. RJam's Gary Smith is secret brother to the men of the suburban chambers of commerce, sharing their worries about cash flow, overhead, and the enforceability of his contracts; but Gary's world and theirs are as far apart as those of Ward and Eldridge Cleaver. Worriers in suburbia fear that ballooning property values will hike taxes on computer executives' seaside homes. In Gary's neighborhood, property values are actually *falling*.

In another sense, of course, the streets surrounding RJam's soundproof studio are the costliest real estate in Boston. At least two young men died as downpayments within a week of today's recording session. Jimmy Carle, 22, a soldier for the Corbet Street gang based south of RJam, was felled by a sniper on the American Legion Highway. This was in retaliation, it's widely rumored, for the Corbet-ordered murder 72 hours before of Roberto Godfrey, 18, leader of a rival gang active in RJam's own North Dorchester. The dead kids plied a trade called retail narcotics, and the mounting body count in Boston's gang war represents a simple application of a cherished chamber of commerce precept: defend your sales territory against competitors.

Gary Smith has competitors too, and he knows RJam lives or dies on the loyalty of its artists. Gary declined a production deal with MCA precisely because he felt it would break faith with performers whose fidelity to the company constitutes RJam's illiquidable inventory. Tam-Tam, today's recordee, is a relatively safe bet in the loyalty department. She considers Gary and Nate Smith family, in part because Nate Smith fathered a child by her older sister. But

9

not all of RJam's artists share Tam-Tam's blood ties to the brothers. Gary Smith knows that the key to the success of his artists lies in getting demo tapes heard by decision-makers at the 20 or so established, if often small, labels that might like the noise and agree to distribute the tape as a record. But, in shopping the tape around, Gary must—like the youth gangs, like anybody in business—be wary. In the rap world, rip-offs are as common as false compliments, and it takes only three minutes to copy a three-minute tape.

Gary's agitated this particular morning by a cut off of girl rapper Antoinette's new LP *Who's the Boss?*. Gary claims that Tam-Tam recorded a slow number called "I'm Cryin" a year ago. The song, which he cues up and plays as he talks, features Tam-Tam, sounding cynical and sexy well beyond her then 15 years, comforting a friend after a breakup; it's a street girl's slam of boys as a whole, a subgenre of rap familiar to fans of Salt-N-Pepa or Neneh Cherry. 'What you crying' for, Pebbles?' Tam-Tam asks her sobbing friend; 'He aint *worth* all that.' A chorus of girls then sings

> *I'm cryyyyyyyyyyyyyyyin*
> *Over you. . . .*

Soon after "I'm Cryin" was done, Tam-Tam herself broke with her partner, the last of several girls to rap with Tam-Tam under the name 'Pebbles.' 'She was making me sound bad,' Tam-Tam would explain this afternoon.

According to Gary, two rival producers liked "I'm Cryin" and offered to buy it. Tam-Tam refused, not because she didn't believe in selling out, rather because she didn't believe in selling out for the few hundred bucks the producers offered. "I'm Cryin" was personal, after all. Tam-Tam spent weeks working out her rhymes.

'That song was *mine*,' she says later. Gary Smith claims, with the pride of a Medici, that "I'm Cryin" was cowritten by one of the backup singers, herself inspired by having Gary break her heart. The song was *his* too.

A few months later, the rival producers dismantled their Boston operation and moved to New York City, selling some of their equipment to RJam but keeping hundreds of demo tapes they'd made or copied, including Tam-Tam's. The two were rumored to have a shadowy 'production deal' with a major label, or with a minor label that itself had a deal with a major label. Months passed before Next Plateau Records released Antoinette's *Who's the Boss?*, featuring a cut called "I'm Cryin," rapped by Antoinette and backed by voices sounding, gosh, an awful lot like Tam-Tam's, singing

I'm cryyyyyyyyyyyyyyyin
Over you....

The bad news came to Tam-Tam over the radio. 'The girls were *hurt* when they heard that song,' Gary recalls. 'They came to see me in the studio. They were *crying*.' Here Gary imitates women crying.

A lawsuit is contemplated, but who can wait for court-ordered justice? Tam-Tam's DJ and producers will today cut the rhythm tracks for a revenge single, aimed at the shameless, plagiarizing Antoinette, under the working title "Ho, You're Guilty."

℘

Gary Smith crosses Geneva Avenue in North Dorchester at the wheel of the leased Chevy Blazer RJAM1, talking shop with Reese

Thomas, Tam-Tam's DJ. Reese was once famous down here as DJ Scratch until a member of Long Island's rap outfit EPMD began using the name. Now Reese is DJ Reese. He, too, is linked to RJam's extended family: his first cousin is Nate Smith's best friend and silent partner, Bobby Brown.

Like the men who invented rap in the Bronx a decade ago, Reese broke in throwing parties for strangers who paid $5/head to bop to his mixology. He and a few buddies rhymed to Public Enemy instrumentals until Reese got bored and began mixing his own rhythm tracks on a battered six-track cassette recorder, using bits and chunks of store-bought music he admired. Soon Reese had a second side business customizing tracks for amateur rappers as he and his friends had once rapped to Def Jam / CBS's Public Enemy. Reese had crossed the rap-blurred line between performer and one-man record company.

Reese's ambition, he says minutes after meeting you, is to have something to do — either as DJ or producer — with the first Boston rap act signed by a 'major label.' Somebody points out that Dorchester's own Gang Starr have just released a well-received LP, *No More Mr. Nice Guy.*

'Yeah,' Reese says, 'but that's not on a *major* label. I'm talking about a *major* label. What label they on?'

'Wild Pitch,' Gary Smith says after thinking about it.

'That's not a major label,' Reese says. He has agreed to produce a rap record for Bobby Brown's sister in coming weeks, his best shot yet at fulfilling his major-label ambitions.

Reese loads a cassette of the rhythm tracks he's worked up for "Ho, You're Guilty" into RJAM1's deck. It's a dense, funky groove.

'Sounds nice,' Gary says. Then he frowns, hearing something. 'What's *that?*' he asks Reese.

'A little help,' Reese says. Meaning that Reese, incorrigible cultural guerilla, has heard a lick he liked in some other rap record and spliced it into what will be the backbone of Tam-Tam's attack on the plagiarizing Antoinette.

'Sample,' Gary says, tsk-tsking. Of such borrowing—called sampling—much rap is made, and nobody but a dunce or Antoinette's lawyers would equate Reese's lifting of ten beats with what RJam claims is the bold wholesale theft of "I'm Cryin." But still, Gary has detected the sample; and the artists sampled, if "Ho, You're Guilty" ever graces rap radio, will detect the sample too. The rap industry is abuzz with news that the Beastie Boys have been sued by funkist Jimmy Castor for their unauthorized re-use of beat and vocal fragments from Castor's "The Return of Leroy (Part I)." De La Soul, whose *3 Feet High and Rising* is considered by many rappers an artistic breakthrough of *Finnegans Wake* proportions, was sued not once but twice over samples on the album. Other suits will surely follow.

Gary, the smart businessman, frowns at the wheel of the Chevy Blazer. But not long. Reese's 'rough draft' cassette sounds too good.

℈

Waiting less than patiently for Tam-Tam, Gary honks twice. A tall, grave girl with an angel's heart-shaped face crosses the ghetto street and climbs into the backseat of RJAM1. She has, apparently, at least two voices: the cynical, sexy rant heard on tape this morning telling Pebbles men aint worth it, and the whisper in which she now says hello.

As RJAM1 recrosses North Dorchester, heading back to the soundproof studios to get the day's work started, Gary and DJ Reese hash out production details. Tam-Tam's a dignified island in the backseat, and a shiver accompanies the thought that this could be the Motor City in '63 with Berry Gordy and an 80-pound teenage Diana Ross, just voted Best Dressed at Cass Technical High School, driving crosstown to record a little number called "Where Did Our Love Go."

Ask Tam-Tam about Diana Ross, and she gives a beatific smile. She's sixteen; she can remember only with difficulty the first rap she ever listened to, when rap was new and she was eight, Run-DMC or somebody, she mumbles in response to what suddenly seems a foolish question about her influences. Like most of rap's black audience (as distinct from rap's white audience, which is usually a decade older), Tam-Tam has no firsthand recollection of James Brown except as a source for rap. She is too young to have attended segregated schools. She was in diapers during the violent first few months of desegregation in Boston and can't remember the awful day in '74 when 'pro-neighborhood' marchers from Irish South Boston came upon a black pedestrian at City Hall and beat him with pole-mounted American flags.

Tam-Tam has star presence, and, like many who do, she seems to see very little of what goes on around her, the price of the star's intense focus on self. She reminds you of Senator Gary Hart. He, too, had star presence. In front of a crowd, Hart was riveting; in the elevator riding up to the auditorium, he was barely there.

Being barely there in the neighborhood Tam-Tam calls home is probably not such a bad thing, and perhaps her drive to be a star someday is an elaborate way to wall out the now and here. Ambition is, finally, a form of hope, a scarce commodity in North Dorchester. Black hopes were raised a couple of elections ago by a ballot item proposing that Roxbury, 8% white, secede from Boston as a new municipality to be named Mandela, Massachusetts. White liberals, feeling jilted, were quick to make apocalyptic predictions about

14

Mandela's inadequate tax base, pointing out, too, that the division of the City into a Black- and a White- was the defeated dream of the old obstructionist school committees dominated by pols named Kerrigan, Tierney, and Leary, St. Patrick's Day demagogues in the John F. Fitzgerald tradition. To some black activists, it sounded as if their old liberal allies were saying that blacks couldn't manage a city of their own, also a favorite theme of Kerrigan, Tierney, and Leary. The whole ugly spat wound up on *Phil Donahue*. The Mandela initiative was beaten, latest in a long line of failed reform schemes.

For generations, Black Boston was promised that places like North Dorchester would get better when the schools improved, and that the schools would improve when integrated. 'Education,' Chief Justice Warren wrote in *Brown*

> ... is the very foundation of good citizenship. Today it is the principal instrument in awakening the child to cultural values, in preparing him for later professional training, and in helping him adjust to his environment. In these days, it is doubtful that any child may reasonably be expected to succeed in life if he is denied the opportunity of an education.... To separate Negro children from others of similar age and qualifications solely because of their race generates a feeling of inferiority as to their status in the community that may affect their hearts and minds in a way unlikely ever to be undone.

Segregation may affect their hearts and minds, Earl Warren warned, as Malcolm X and Louis Farrakhan, both alumni of Boston's old separate-but-awful schools, bear loud witness. Now, 40 years after X disgustedly quit a racist high school and began a career as a kind of bebop gangbanger, 35 years after *Brown v. Board of Education* invented integration, 15 years after *Morgan v. Hennigan* brought *Brown* to Boston, North Dorchester is worse and its schools aren't better. A former United States Secretary of Education converts to Drug Czar, symbolizing a national change of mind: now drugs, not poor schools (and certainly not the American apartheid of which segregated schools were but one facet), are our root 'inner-city' problem. Tam-Tam's Boston is strangely less hopeful than the notoriously segregated pre-*Hennigan* city, perhaps because before *Hennigan,* reformers could promise that segregation was why things were so bad. Segregation was blame's bull's-eye: abolish the bull's-eye, and blame for the estrangement of the races flies everywhere, hitting the cops, or the courts, or the teachers, or the taught, or what's taught. There's even a rap—B.D.P.'s "Why Is That?"—blaming our miseries on the failure of the schools to 'teach black kids to be black.'

Most of the blame for Tam-Tam's world is currently, officially hung on drugs and on the youth gangs that traffic drugs. The Boston Police Department has managed to target blame even more exactly, asserting that much of the crack on the streets of this city is shipped here by Jamaica-connected mobsters who muscled into the lucrative Boston market after paying for the killing of the one man who blocked their entrance.

That man was Tony C. Johnson, 22, reputed boss of the Corbets, in its heyday Boston's strongest gang. Police say Johnson had organized the city's biggest posses into a loose union whose aim was to keep the Jamaicans out of Roxbury/Mandela. Johnson's union lasted a year, until a night in June '87, when the charismatic leader was beheaded by multiple blasts from a sawed-off 12-gauge as he parked his mother's car on a street not far from Tam-Tam's building.

A manhunt for Johnson's killers ensued, and a pair of young hoods—William Samuels, then 20, and Paul Larry Guild, then 19—were charged. With Johnson gone, the B.P.D. theory runs, crack could be dealt freely, and crack is blame's new bull's-eye. The theory puts staggering onus on Johnson's assassins, Samuels and Guild. The two were unlikely Oswalds when, police believe, an emissary from the Jamaicans (true kingpins, dwarfing even Johnson; men who dealt, literally, in eight figures) made them the once-in-a-lifetime murder-for-hire offer. Guild and Samuels's options in Boston: the Army; or the minimum wage; or careers in muggings, burglaries, possessions with intent; stints at the Commonwealth's minimum-security facility on Deer Island in Boston Harbor, forestalled perhaps by informing on close friends; then the medium-security pen at Dedham; then, finally, when busted for a big enough felony or sentenced to life under Massachusetts's habitual offender statute, a long stay at the 'Hard Rock Café,' maximum-security Walpole, from which they'd emerge middle-aged, professional prisoners. A cheerless prospect to consider at 19.

Then came the offer from the Jamaicans, a career fork faced a few years back by Eazy-E of the controversial rap group N.W.A. Eazy-E made a figurative killing dealing dope, but considered life in the gangs a poor long-run proposition. 'I decided to look for something legal to do with the money I'd made,' he told the *L.A. Times*. Bankrolled by gangstering, Eazy-E in '86 founded Ruthless Records, a pioneering rap production company.

Maybe rap as an alternative to desultory criminal obscurity didn't occur to the assassins Samuels and Guild. Perhaps their plan was to collect the price on Johnson's head and retire in style to Brazil. But perhaps, like Eazy-E, they dreamed of investing their big payday in studio time at RJam, of cutting a rap LP that would sell 700,000 copies like Eazy-E's solo effort *Eazy-Duz-It.* Either way, killing Tony Johnson was their ticket out. Either way, the hit would make them stars.

And best of luck making sense out of gangbanging, out of rap, out of anything in Reaganania or this book without admitting first that the hub of the wheel is the urge to be a star. Why did Tawana Brawley insist for a year that she'd been raped by a gang of whites? Because she told the lie to begin with; and lies, once told, are easier to extend than end. Why did she tell the lie to begin with? Probably because she wanted attention. Like the teenage Diana Ross, she wanted to be a star. In this respect, the Tawana Brawley phenomenon is a haunting mix of Linda Brown — the Topeka child plaintiff who claimed that a white gang called the Board of Education held her hostage in a segregated school system — and the Salem witch complainants — who were themselves about Tawana Brawley's age when they claimed that they were transported to the woods and stuck repeatedly with pins. Like the Salem witch complainants, Tawana Brawley entered the confusions of puberty in a time of paranoia. Now spokesmen for Ms. Brawley tell the *New York Daily News* that she would like to be an actress someday. And if the Salem Seven lived in a teenybopping era, they too could segue into showbiz, forming the Salemettes, white-skinned Supremes with necessarily more complicated dance steps, singing, *Here I am, signed, sealed, delivered, I'm yours.*

Fear of devils is not limited to teenagers, and neither is the stardom urge. The difference between the adolescent's need to be noticed and the big star's need to be even bigger is equipment: begging *Look what I've done,* L.L. Cool J raps that he started out in his basement and now is double platinum, a boast that *itself* goes double platinum.

☙

Back in RJam's control booth, DJ Reese and producer Ralph Stacey are programming the rhythm track for what will be "Ho, You're Guilty." Drum parts are taken from a Roland TR-909 Rhythm Composer, a synth that electronically reproduces programmed beats on the user's choice of drum matrix. The TR-909's keys, on a console designed to resemble, vaguely, the familiar piano, are named after the sound each creates—bass, snare, mid-tom, hi-tom—and the sounds are named after the actual drums that, until the TR-909, were required to make those sounds. The TR-909 even sports a key named HAND CLAP, making it possible for the first time ever to clap hands with a single finger, forever outmoding Zen koans about the sound of one hand clapping. The finished "Ho, You're Guilty" will sound lush with percussion, melody, and instrumental breaks. Not one human musician will be employed in the recording process.

Each percussion line is programmed onto the mixing board as a separate track: a snare track, a bass track, a clap track, etc. Reese has been studying the classics lately too, viz.: James Brown's *Dead on the Heavy Funk* from 1975ish, including the ageless groove "Funky President," in which James announces his third-party candidacy. Some of Bobby Byrd's *Dead* guitar, and a holy moment when James exhales rhythmically, have been isolated from a store-bought cassette of *Dead,* rerecorded on clean tape, then rererecorded onto a computer-readable memory diskette from which the sample is retrieved and altered by Ralph Stacey using a Roland D-50 linear synth. The guitar and the exhalation then go, as altered, from the synth to yet another of the 24 tracks on the big mixing board. Reese, the DJ, will weave a seamless rhythm track out of these 24 strands.

As Reese and Ralph Stacey mix the 24 tracks onto one master tape, Tam-Tam sips lemonade in the corner of the booth. You ask her if she is interested someday in learning about the obscure digital technology the two men manipulate on her behalf. She doesn't seem to register the question. 'The other career [besides rap] I'd like to pursue is modeling,' she says. 'I'm 5'7". That's the perfect height for a model.'

Mixing takes the rest of the day. Producer Ralph Stacey at one late point corners you with a flinty stare and an uncomfortable question: 'Why do *you* want to write about rap, anyway?' It is lucky that at that minute Reese is done mixing. Tomorrow RJam staff will tape Tam-Tam's vocal track and lay this over Reese's rhythm track. Then the sound will be 'fattened' with stacks of horns, guitar hooks, bells, canned applause, and whatever else they decide to take from other tapes or work up on the Roland. The final demo tape of "Ho, You're Guilty" will then be shopped to the 20 major, minor, and tiny labels that might release the demo as a 12-inch single.

Everyone's ready to call it a day. Gary Smith's already huddled with some new wannabe-stars in RJam's reception area. Reese plays the mixed rhythm track once through over the big speakers in the control booth, and Tam-Tam immediately stands, modeling forgotten, utterly alert. Reese gestures to her with maestro hands. She raps at an absent Antoinette in the hard, sexy voice you haven't heard since this morning, extemporaneous but on beat:

> *I'm a female*
> *You're just a fairytale.*

D.

(1B)

PRODUCER STACEY'S QUESTION 'Why do _you..._?' persists, booms. Who on earth's entitled to declaim about light-sources too far out to get to? Well, anybody. The night sky's spray of light is there, at a distance, for anyone to see and invoke. The heavens, that best chiaroscuro, are color-blind. Not so culture, race in the U.S. present. Please know we're very sensitive to this question: what business have two white yuppies trying to do a sampler on rap? Don't of course think we're really yuppies. We two are emphatically _not_ yuppies. 'Yuppie' is a predicate exclusively mass-, one conceived by demographers for use by marketers, as in _Bright Lights,_ "Built for the Human Race," "Material Girl," _thirtysomething,_ "The Night Belongs to Michelob," "You Can Have It All." No one's a yuppie because _everyone's_ a yuppie, a consummate consumer, for U.S. purposes, today. Even — you will not leave this sampler unconvinced — that unlikeliest of markets, black recording artists on the leading edge of the pop explosion called rap: yuppiness right out their dactylic assonance, shouting at the tops of their trochee'd rhymes across an impenetrable emptiness that they are *there, here,* here-and-now: like Us in their self-conscious difference, their congregation at the altar of electronic Self; with Us in their alien hate; at the deepest level one with the yuppie U.S.

The small-w 'we' here are two white Boston males: one native, one oft-transplanted; both residing in 'Somer-bridge,' a dim, ethnic-Portuguese neighborhood whose gentrification we abet; of comfortably nervous two-income parents; products of the sorts of schools Barron's sells books trying to get you into. M. is an attorney with a taste for jazz, Blues, funk; D. a grad student and would-be drifter who watches TV instead of sleeping, is coming more and more to prefer the commercials to the shows, and listens with half a faithful ear to pretty much whatever cheese product the Boston station he's too lazy to change is processing this hour. Our cultural tastes and interests are day and night. They converged only lately, when D.'s stereo arrived UPS and we discovered we shared an uncomfortable, somewhat furtive, and distinctively white enthusiasm for a certain music called rap/hip-hop.[1] About our passions and discomforts we could determine only that they were vague & distinct contexts and cathexes brought to bear across the same ethnic distance on the same thing. For instance we agreed that real or serious rap is not J.J.

---

[1]"Hip-hop"'s an older synonym, coined by rap pioneer Kool Herc to describe the heavily danceable Jamaican scatting he introduced between records at the huge South Bronx block parties he and other new-Scene celebrities, like Jazzy Five and former Black Spades leader Afrika Bambaataa, could turn into late-'70s frenzies of Breakdance (both music and dance a self-conscious reaction against the glittered unreality of downtown Disco).

Fad or Tone Lōc or Beasties, Egyptian Lover or Fat Boys, not experiments or freakshows or current commercial crossover slush. 'Serious' rap—a unique U.S. inner-city fusion of funk, technified reggae, teen-to-teen 'hardcore' rock, and the early '70s' 'poetry of the black experience' of Nikki Giovanni, the Last Poets, etc.—has, since its late-'70s delivery at the record-scratching hands of Afrika Bambaataa and his Zulu Nation, Sugarhill Gang, Kool Herc and his automated Herculords, and Grandmaster Flash, always had its real roots in the Neighborhood, the black gangbanger Underground, like trees over septics. Black music, of and for blacks.

We concurred as to the wheres and whens of rap's begetting— mid- to late-'70s South Bronx house parties; then, by decade's end, block parties, with municipal electric lights tapped for a power source, literal dancing in the streets; by '82 regular rap houses and then 'floating clubs'—the Roxy every Sunday, the Bronx's Disco Fever TWTh—everybody Breaking to a new musical antimusic being fashioned from records and turntables and an amateur DJ's ad-lib banter; a very heavy reggae influence at the beginning; the more rhythmic pure rap an offshoot, its brisker sparer backbeat designed for Breakdance (Kool Herc: 'We just discovered our own drum machines in scratching the records') and the smooth-rapping partygoer who just didn't want to shut up when others' music was on. We agreed, too, on rough chronology: amateur house-partiers giving way to professional DJs, pioneers; they too then overshadowed by new art-entrepreneurs, former Breakers, failed singers, gang majorettes; then the rise of 'Indies,' the tiny independent labels that keep most new musics on life support—Sugar Hill, Jive, Tommy Boy, Wild Pitch, Profile Records, Enjoy—then, after King Tim III's "Personality Jock" and Sugarhill Gang's "Rapper's Delight," an entré into urban black radio; then to underground

'Mix' radio; then corporate labels, digital technology, very big money, the early-'80s' talent that became an early Scene's cream — Spoonie Gee and Sequence, Eric Fresh, Unknown DJ, Egyptian Lover and Run-DMC. Then, spring '84, the extraordinary Midas touch of Rick Rubin and Russell Simmons's Def Jam label (now under contract to CBS) from which sprang a mid-'80s stable of true stars, in the Underground—Public Enemy, L.L. Cool J, Slick Rick—and L.A.'s alternatives: Ice T, L.A. Dream Team, others. And now, in the '90s' early light, an absolute explosion of rap-as-pop, big business, MTV, special fashions, posters, merchandise, with only a few big new cutting-edge acts—L.A.'s N.W.A, Philadelphia's Schoolly D, Miami's 2 Live Crew, De La Soul's House blend of rap/funk/jazz—remaining too esoteric or threatening or downright obscene to cross all the way over and cash in with big labels. By '90 rap is finally proving as 'Important' (read also Lucrative) to an anemic shock- and rebellion-music industry as Punk was an exact decade ago. This was all just data. We agreed on it, and on how it was curious that we both had such strange, distant facts down cold.

Our point of departure, essay-wise, was always less what we knew than what we felt, listening; less what we liked than why. For this attempt at an outside sampler we plunked down and listened to thousands of hours of rap, trying to summon a kind of objective, critical, purely 'aesthetic' passion that the music itself made impossible. For outsiders, rap's easy to move to, hard to dissect. The more we listened and thought and drank beers and argued, the more we felt that the stuff's appeal for two highbrow upscale whites was just plain incongruous. Because serious rap has, right from the start, presented itself as a Closed Show. Usually, critical questions of culture, context, background, and audience reduce quickly to vexed questions about prepositions. Not here. No question that serious rap is, and is very self-consciously, music *by* urban blacks *about* same *to* and *for* same. And, weirdly, all these prepositions and indirect objects remain identical for the many 'Underground' rappers who are each month, now, captured and contracted by the big white-run recording corps. There's an aura of cohesion-in-competition, of an exclusive and shared universe in the present rap relationship between black artists and black audience not enjoyed by a music especially of and for people of color in something like the last 80 years.[2] To mainstream whites it's a tight cohesion that can't but look, from outside the cultural window, like occlusion, clannishness [sic], and inbreeding, a kind of reverse snobbery about what's 'def' and 'fresh' and in-the-Scene that eerily recalls the exclusionary codes of college Societies and WASP-only country clubs. Serious rap's a musical movement that seems to revile whites as a group or Establishment and simply to ignore their possibility as distinct individuals—the Great White Male is rap's Grand Inquisitor, its idiot questioner, its Alien Other no less than Reds were for McCarthy. The music's paranoia, together with its hermetic racial context, maybe helps explain why it appears just as vibrant and impassioned as it does alien and scary, to us, from outside.

Other incongruities. Rap is a 'music' essentially without melody, built instead around a digitally synthesized drum- and backbeat often about as complex as five idle fingers on a waiting-room table, enhanced by 'sampled' (pirated) 'krush grooves' (licks or repetitive chord series) conceived and recorded by pre-rap rock icons, the whole affair comprised by a distinctive, spare, noisy, clattering 'style' whose obsessive if limited thematics revolve with the speed of low-I

---

[2] *Dance Music* magazine's Volume 12 #11, a special issue on rap, calls the genre: 'The purest, freshest form of black expression since early jazz.'

amperage around the performative circuit of the MC/rapper and his record-scratching, sound-mixing Sancho Panza, the DJ.

The rapper (the guy in the cameo cut or Kangol hat, pricey warm-up, unlaced Adidas, extra-thick gold chain or oversized medallion) offers lyrics that are spoken or bellowed in straight stressed rhymed verse, the verse's syntax and meter often tortured for rhythmic gain or the kind of limboing-for-rhyme we tend to associate with doggerel about men from Nantucket. The lyrics, nearly always self-referential, tend to be variations on about half a dozen basic themes, themes that at first listen can seem less alien or shocking than downright dull. E.g.: just how bad/cool/fresh/def the rapper and his lyrics are; just how equally un–all these his musical rivals are; how troublesome, vacuous, and acquisitive women are; how wonderful it is to be 'paid in full' for rapping instead of stealing or dealing; how gangs are really families, and 'caine's constant bad news. And, in particular, how sex and violence and yuppie toys represent perfectly the urban black lifedrive to late-'80s American glory. (This latter many older blacks despise as less dull than just a disgusting recidivism to a pre–King/Malcolm vision, like your kid pawning your Purple Heart to buy rubbers and gin.)

The MC's Alice Toklas–esque DJ hovers ever nearby over his buffet of connected turntables and the black Germanness of a whole lot of digital editing & playback equipment. His responsibility is the song behind and around the rap — the backbeat, krush groove, and the 'sound carpet,' i.e., a kind of electric aural environment, a chaos behind the rapper's rhymed order, a digitalized blend of snippets, squeaks, screams, sirens, snatches from pop media, all mixed and splattered so that the listener cannot really listen but only *feel* the mash of 'samples' that results. The most recognizable of these samples range from staccato record scratches to

James Brown and Funkadelic licks, to MLK's public Dream, to quotidian pop pap like the "Theme from *Shaft*," *Brady Bunch* dialogue, and '50s detergent commercials.

Frequently, the DJ is also the rapper's foil, offering rap refrains, or sometimes replies to the rapper's verses in the genre's use of the venerable convention of 'call and response,' often speaking in rhythmless prose against the rapper's complexly metered rhyme. The Mozart of this last technique is Public Enemy's shadow-MC Flavor Flav, who holds his head cocked like Stevie Wonder and wears an alarm clock the size of a dinner plate around his neck, ad-libbing exhortations to Public Enemy MC Chuck D to

> *Let them know who's who and where in the world we'll be*
> *You gots to tell them that this is the '80s*
> *And we can get all the ladies*
> *And in the backyard we got a fine Mercedes*
> *And that's just the way the story goes....*

Sometimes, though, the rapper is just too cool to need any homeboy's response to his call, as in

> *Look at what I've done*
> *Used to rap in my basement, now I'm Number 1*
> *And just gettin busier*
> *I'm double platinum, I'm watchin' you get dizzier....*

in a typical 'Soft rap' from L.L. Cool J, Number 1 fan of his own success and general panache.

Or sometimes the rapper's self-conscious enough to serve as his own responder, as in Def Jam mogul/manager/rapper Russell

'Rush' Simmons's pre-bridge rap to "Cold Chillin' in the Spot" on the B side of one of his label's early singles

> *This is the B side of a record called* Def Jam
> *Now bridge, let's go to the bridge...*

...Or else just too frankly nasty for anyone even to want to be around him, as in N.W.A's

> *You know I spell 'Girl' with a 'B'*
> *And a brother like me's only out for one thing*
> *I think with my dingaling...*
> *You want lobster?*
> Hah. *I'm thinkin' Burger King*
> *And after the date you know I'll want to do the wildest thing*
> *...I got what I wanted—now beat it.*

from MC Ice Cube, who earlier on N.W.A's *Straight Outta Compton* serves as prosecuting attorney in the capital trial of an L.A. patrolman for 'the crime of being a white-bread chickenshit mothafucka.'

The prenominate quotations and assessments may seem harsh, unsympathetic. By and large they're mild compared to the sort of mainstream rock criticism's view of serious rap we kept encountering as we tried to secondary-source our way toward an understanding of wheel's hub, incongruous allure, verbal entitlement.

Grant us at least secondary authority. We have now read every review and essay to do with serious underground hip-hop available in every single on-line periodical...except for one or two underground newsletters (viz. *Rapmasters, FreshEst*) circulated in parts of the Bronx demimonde where learning about rap is as hard for white outsiders as scoring fine China White or AKs. From the kind of sedulous biblio-maniacal research to be expected of conscientious lawyers and pre-Ph.D.'s, the following has become clear. Outside England, where the Punk-weaned audience has developed a taste for spectacle-through-windows, for vicarious Rage and Protest against circum-stances that have exactly 0% to do with them, most of what *Rolling Stone* calls 'devoted rock consumers' (meaning we post–baby boom-ers), plus almost *all* established rock critics, tend to regard serious, ever new, non-crossover rap as essentially boring and simplistic, or as swaggering and bellicose and dangerous, at all events as basically vapid and empty because of its obsessive self-referentiality... in short, as *closed* to them, to Us, as a music. It's unrecognizable as what we've been trained and adverted to buy as pop.... Great to *dance* to, of course, but then what might the white audience for today's main-stream expect?—for rap, whether fecund or sterile, is today's pop music's lone cutting edge, the new, the unfamiliar, the brain-resisted-while-body-boogies. And that resisted, alien, exhilarating cutting edge has always been black, and always an augury of pop's every near-future, since everything we now recognize and salivate on cue over in the white teen and yuppie mass-market rock and dance world was invented by, then bought or bit from, an insular or regional, highly time-and-place-dependent black music scene, from swaying spirituals and front-porch minor fifths off baling wire[3] to Dix, jazz, Blues, soul, James Brown, Motown, Jimi Hendrix, and the '70s' funk innovations of Clinton's Parliament & Hayes & their votaries, to (umm) disco, then late-'70s dance-funk, Break, and now hip-hop/rap.

The Spike Lee–directed video for Public Enemy's "Fight the

---

[3]Early Blues history reports Chess Records' legendary Chess brothers schlepping out into Mississippi cotton fields to recruit promising artists on their lunch breaks.

Power" has the band leading a re-enactment of MLK's 1963 March on Washington, with then NYC mayor Koch and economic inequality the bones to be picked. In the wake of the April '89 Central Park rape and the Manhattan scourge of 'wilding' (necklace-snatching and convenience-store trashing) by prepubescent black Brooklynites dressed as L.L. Cool J—wannabes, the media has begun in earnest to link rap music with 'antisocial' behavior in editorials more than eerily reminiscent of establishment/critical reaction to early Elvis, Bill Haley, Gene Vincent, et al., when the stakes and temperatures were so much lower. *Eminence noire* Afrika Bambaataa guest-writes in *Dance Music:* 'A reflection of social conditions, the expression of anger and frustration, music constructed with basic elements at hand have always been present in some form in black music. Even earliest Gospel and Blues included narratives and bare beat-backed spoken words.' Etc. It's more than arguable now that, in the serious rap Scene, black music's American history is come weirdly full circle. For, like that music's earliest incarnations—spirituals and one-wire Blues—its latest presents itself as proudly crude, shaped by nothing but genius and what is at hand, homemade by and for special pockets of (once rural, now terribly urban) privation;[4] and, by dint both of the economic circumstances of its nascence and of its consciously promulgated political design, as *not for Us,* not directed to the sort of audience (homogeneous, mostly middle-class white, highly sensitive to the shepherd's whistle of Market) one normally

---

[4] Though note that certain paradoxes inherent in the new massive national popularity & profitability of today's rap—discussed ad nauseam below—render rap's original crude or homemade character now largely an image, a conscious artistic choice; the earliest U.S. black music's minimalist, patchwork qualities were aesthetically more straightforward for the simple reason that they were functions of actual *constraint* (as was rap's infancy) rather than of image or representation.

associates with precious-metal records and Fad's combustion into Movement or 'Wave.' Rap's highly self- and history-conscious unfamiliarity, its image of inaccessibility to established markets or truly teeming-mass appeal, is often reduced by critics to the kind of 'surly musical hostility'[5] that, like Punk's, quickly loses its novelty for those outside, can become for Us like little more than looking at something poisonous in a tightly closed jar.

Except who exactly sealed the lid, this time? The mainstream record reviewer? He's but Market's bitchy mistress. The Market itself—Us? But *everything* the white rock listener pays to enjoy is black-begotten. If today's Top 40 environment seems bleak or befouled, imagine the present mainstream without its sweetest source waters, without the King-Waters-King Blues trinity, the Brownian soul, the backbeat, cut time, blue notes, funky French curves of sex and brass, the guitar solo, call-and-response, the Cold Medina or Lucky Powder, those lithely syncopated quintets in Pomade and linen suits, the single hand in the white glove holding Pepsi aloft in the shadow of accidental flames.... Black music is American pop's breath and bread; and We, as both born audience and born salesmen, know it.

So maybe it's them. *Them.* Maybe we're approaching an enforced fork in the musical road where the white-run entertainment industry will have to pack up what it's taken and go seek its future's fortune on the backs of new minorities. Maybe, in serious rap, the extreme new insulation of the black sound is not only intentional but *preplanned,* part of a neo-Nationalist, my God near-National-*Socialist* agenda, the hermetic new Scene's tight circle more like something large coiled than something small flat.

You may now be getting some hazy idea of the sorts of really

---

[5] Redundancy sic, the *New York Times,* 21 May 1989, 'A&E,' p. 23.

quite scary possibilities with which the rap we like is replete. And, hazier, of how complicated this stuff of sampler-from-outside can be. What's remained passing strange, for us, is rap's vague threat's *appeal.* The unease and ambivalence with which the rare white at the window loves rap renders that love no less love. Is this perverse? A kind of extra-expensive yuppie masochism? No-pain-no-gain type of deal?... Or like chasing after the girl not despite but *because of* the fact she wants no part of you—especially *that* part?

Whence the fear, though, is really no matter. For look at the world, at the masses we're part of. At what you look at closest. The late-millennial data indicate clearly that, whereas love, devotion, passion, seem only to divide, it's fear and strangeness that now bind crowds, fill halls, unite Us, somehow, as audience, under the great tent.

E.g., on the occasions when rap's new musical focus—its spoken lyrics—prove most genuinely engaging to *both* the jaded B-boy (who loathes the Tone Lōc whites tend to find so cute 'n' cuddly) *and* the white-establishment listener (of whom I consider myself a fine example and rep., and I have to admit to an extra-Scenic, caucasian contempt for L.L. Cool J's and Slick Rick's bantam-cock Songs of Themselves that so regularly top black charts), to B-boy and white boy alike, it's usually because there's this 'something vague' coiled in those lyrics, inviting fear. For the B-boy on the Scene, the fear's been described as of the gritty & grainy yet also terribly mythic depiction of projects' and ghettos' special hells, the crack house[6] and drive-by, the insecurity and pain in a here-and-now pumped artistically up to where it seems everywhere and evermore. For the white, behind his transparent cultural impediment, though,

---

[6] (which a Minneapolis rap set yr. staff spoke with kept calling 'the church of very short prayers')

the Hard rap begins in mood to resemble something more like temblor, epiclesis, *prophecy:* it's not like good old corporate popular art, whose job was simply to remind us of what we already know; issues of all kinds of distance enter in and complicate the rap matter, from outside, fear-wise. To judge from record and ticket sales, the best rap records for young whites are the violently political or 'Hard' raps that are so much like getting fake-flogged by a mime, a for-art's-sake dressing-down *full* of contempt and parody and vague menace... but all from the other side of a chasm we feel glad, if liberal-guilty, is there: some *space* between our own lawned split-level world and whatever it is that lends the authenticity[7] to Schoolly D's thuggish rip-offs of '70s mainstream classics; or to Chuck D's full-throated Farrakhanesque 'positions,' orated before Public Enemy's infamous background of electric angst-bagpipes and a sound carpet sampled by X and by media-savvy, militant Black Muslim 'Professor Griff' and laid back down so densely it's the garbled white noise that means dead channel...; or, say, to N.W.A's

> *Ice Cube will swarm*
> *On any mothafucka in a blue uniform*
> *A young nigger on the warpath*
> *And when I finish*
> *It's going to be a bloodbath*
> *Of cops, dying in L.A.*[8]

or to the sneering white-hate in Ice T's unlikely million-selling crossover hit from the movie *Colors*

---

[7] (described best by the archaic adj. 'soul')
[8] From '89's "Fuck tha Police."

Tell me what have you left me, what have I got?
Last night in cold blood my young brother got shot
My homey got jacked
My mother's on crack
My sister can't work 'cause her arms show tracks
Madness, insanity
Live in profanity
Then some punk claim that they understandin' me?
Give me a break — what world do you live in?
Death is my sex — guess my religion.[9]

What makes this stuff so much more disturbing, more *real* to outsiders than the Punk rock even those of us who remember it could never quite take seriously? Maybe even a closed music has to have some kind of détente with received custom: I always found it tough to listen straight-faced to a nihilist-philosophy lecture from someone with a chartreuse mohawk and an earring in his eyelid who punctuated with vomit and spit. All doctrine and pronouncement, exclusively anti-, this Punk of a decade past afforded even willing mainstream listeners no easement across cultural void, nothing human to grab on to. I have no idea what a Punk performer thinks, feels, *is*, day-to-day...in fact always suspected he *had* no day, but just retreated to his plush coffin at cock's crow. Can

---

[9] Except but now hey kids! thanks to AT&T you can now speak directly to Ice T and hear his philosophy of life by phone! 1-900-907-9111. 'Chill out with Ice T,' the rapper, adrape in military hardware and ammunition, says on MTV; 'I'm just waiting on you to call me,' pointing at the camera and then himself lest the audience get at all confused. 'Don't forget to ask your parents' permission first' (white corporate voice-over) — $2.00 first minute, etc. etc.

you imagine a Punk with four-foot hair and spiked jacket and nose ring, say, eating a bologna sandwich? replacing a lightbulb? putting a quarter in a meter? Not me, boy. And even Barnum, who knew fear sells, also knew that freak shows aren't frightening when the freakishness supplants all resemblance. 0% affinity = 0% empathy. And fear requires empathy as much as it does menace or threat.

Public Enemy and N.W.A, Ice T and Schoolly D discomfit us, our friends, the critics we read and cornered, because the Hard rappers' lyrics are conscientious about being of/for the real lives and attitudes of recognizable (if alien) *persons*. Here's where it's a level up from mere spectacle: ideology in Hard rap's always informed by incident or named condition, and thus anger by cause, threat by some kind of recognizable (to the Scene) provocation. And this makes rap not only better than Punk, but way scarier. Serious Hard raps afford white listeners genuine, horse's-mouth access to the life-and-death plight and mood of an American community on the genuine edge of im-/explosion, an ugly new subnation we've been heretofore conditioned to avoid, remand to the margins, not even *see* except through certain carefully abstract, attenuating filters: cop show and news special, crafted commercial fad, the Bush-appointed Drug Czars and sober editorials we demand as 'Concerned Citizens' deeply concerned about the future of urban districts we might, after all, want to build co-ops in someday.

Rap knows its lyrics, Soft or Hard—to say nothing of the exhilarating dance-till-you-die beats—are a step up from funk and Punk. The music knows its power of salient affect, its overweening relevance and appeal to blacks, and thus its anywhere-but-here place in white mainstream culture; and it knows it knows it; and it shows it in its sincere up-yours attitude toward whatever might homogenize or centralize[10] the music, an attitude that both excites Us and keeps Us at the distance Our excitement depends on, making of the market mainstream a yo-yo on a fickle finger, at rap's beck... and, in another tight loop, rap does all this by keeping the music *closed,* prepositionally black, Other, so that regardless of corporate favor and subsidy it can and must remain a cutting edge... the only kind of edge We fear, anymore, at all.

Rap's fearful attraction for white audiences (though not yet critics) is admittedly twiny. Here's a simple first way to analogize audience affect. Recall that what became the '70s cinematic cliché of Slasher Movies like *Halloween* and *Friday the Thirteenth I–XV* was the 'killer-view shot,' a camera angle via which the audience is forced to follow the grisly action through the slasher's own eyes and so can't help but see victims as he does: prey. Most Hard raps, too, seem to launch themselves through the window toward white listeners as from the point of view of the nighttime footsteps that make us quicken our pace and exert much will not to look back, of the rowdy or sinister-silent groups of B-boys on the platform or corner we'll casually cross streets to avoid. It is, no pun meant, the most street-level view yet of a subcommunity we tend to think we favor by ignoring: the urban black late–baby boom poor who are now (post–Irish/Italian and perhaps pre–Chinese/Korean), finally, America's great *Alien Within,* the carcinomoid Other, inside Us, one whose desperate contemporary condition and response to it—i.e., their daily lives—we Concerned Citizens decry and deplore and

---

[10]We neglected, in [9], to mention that Ice T is snickering and camping all thru his special-Ice-T-line MTV ad, though the fact that he's clearly sneering all the way to the bank puts yet another spin on the who's-exploiting-whom issue. As with anything on MTV, it's probably safe here to assume the viewer's the real exploitee.

target in 'Wars On' AIDS, Crime, Gangs, Crime, Crack, Crime, Homelessness, Illiteracy, Teenage Pregnancy, Low SAT Scores Among College Athletes, Crime, etc.

It's at the distinctively pop-cultural bregma where common-sense polarities like art vs. politics, medium vs. message, center vs. margin conjoin and must cohabit that even an enthusiastic white establishment-cog's try at some 'objective aesthetic appreciation' of rap runs aground. Since rap's self-defined as by and for a group that We, as post-Reagan white culture, regard as Other, it's a music out of which we tend automatically to edit troublesome complexities like individual artists' unique experiences, tastes, beliefs, models, values, and agenda, in order to achieve the wide shallow definition the rubric *Representative Voice of Threatening Alien Culture* imposes. The idiosyncratic, the *person-al*—rich and eccentric and too complex even to see unless you're right there up close—are our attributes *for Us*, not for Aliens, not even Aliens-among-Us. This shouldn't be news, nor should be the fact that much civil rights law walks an uneasy line between trying to enjoin certain types of behavior and trying to enlighten the attitudes behind them, attitudes that tend to be infallible functions of the reduction & simplification of seeing across chasms. *Hennigan,*[11] for example, is ultimately just as much about how people see as it is about where they live or learn, as in

> In Boston the term 'Roxbury' probably carries many
> of the connotations which 'Harlem' does in New York
> City. Unfortunately, streets in disrepair, burned out
> houses left standing, and rubbish left on side streets in

---

[11](the 1974 decision that found the Boston public schools to be a fat bundle of civil rights violations)

parts of Roxbury cannot help but intensify the identification of parts of this section of the city.

But please see that this decoct-and-simplify phenomenon is not necessarily racist, or even specifically rac*ial*. It looks, rather, to be just a phylogenic part of human circuitry...though, since the culture is the basic unit of sameness and difference, the specific context of any simplification is going to be cultural. The important thing is that *it can work both ways,* and from any Outside. Allow me to e.g. concretely. I'm sitting, just the other day, on the front steps of the Widener Library. A group of Japanese tourists—native Japanese, for whom the U.S. of A. might as well be Mars—a group of these tourists approaches, brandishing cameras.

'*Harvard,* please,' one says to me.

I look up from the navel I'm contemplating. 'Excuse me?'

'Where is *Harvard,*' the guy says, the tourists behind him all nodding in very polite earnest.

Well Widener is the central library building of Harvard, in the middle of Harvard Yard, which is itself the geographical heart of H.U. So I kind of cock my head at him and say: 'Well, all around you, this is all Harvard, you've been walking right through it.'

They have a conference. 'But we are looking for *Harvard,*' another finally says to me, with an emphasis that implies I don't get it.

I am nonplussed. Frantic to signify that they're inside what they're looking for, I sort of try to point vaguely in all directions at once.

'HARVARD,' they keep iterating politely, checking a kind of bilingual Japanese *Webster's.*

Turns out, of course, after much semioticizing, that they're looking for just one—any—uniquely identifying Harvard-site, a good old venerable synecdoche, some kind of visual Harvard-souvenir they can photograph and then, back home, in Japan, point to for friends who don't know Harvard from a hole and say: 'Look: *Harvard*.'

Now, accept the analogy between a particular university and a particular community, and the point of this encounter of the cultural kind emerges: for people not in or of it, a community's a *thing*, not a *place*. And it's certainly not an *environment* where separate species in all their differences and complexity mingle and diffract.

Now a joke:

> **Q:** What's the difference between a telescope and a stereotype?
>
> **A:** Depends which end of the 'scope you're looking through.

Now not such a joke, though:

> **Q:** Just what's the difference between a stereotype and a good old venerable synecdoche?

'Synecdoche,' from the Greek *sunekdōkhe,* meaning 'To associate with or understand in terms of another,' and from the Old French *synecdoche/synecdōque,* meaning simply 'It'...both in turn, of course, meaning the conceptual promotion of Part to Whole, a rhetorical thing, as in: 'Give me a HAND with this engine, will you?' or 'That rancher's got 300 HEAD ready for market already,' etc. And I think we all know pretty well what a stereotype is.

So then but what's the difference? It seems like stereotype and synecdoche effect pretty much the same editing-by-mail procedure, pumping a unitary Part up to the representative status of complex Whole; the only real and final difference lies in just how much air's

39

in the pumped-up Part. In life, as in just walking around or sitting there observing and processing, the synecdoche's as inescapable as the retina, basically. And advertisers have clued into this, have canonized the synecdochical process in the sort of supravisual iconography they need to impose the very same association-freighted symbol on millions in a moment. The California Raisins. Domino's Pizza's migrainous Noid. Merrill Lynch's drugged-looking bull; NBC's peacock; a nerd's pocket-protector; a camp queen's lisp and waggle; a mic's red nose. 7-Up's new campaign's new sprightly red Spot, jumping around. Spuds MacKenzie, Nixon's plea for perfect clarity, the Bush-handlers' Dukakis = Horton = Crime triquation. Those nutty Keebler elves. The rappin', jivin', big-dicked, thick-lipped gangbanger B-boy. Etc.[n]

Confession: D.'s first sampler draft, of which this brief digressive riff is a grim fossil, began as more about rap-as-synecdoche than about rap *esse*. For rap *presents* itself as synecdochic: its dual identity as both head and limb, speaking both to and for its audience, is a huge part of the authority it claims in every cut.

Too, the rhetorical relation of Part to Whole symbolizes (and so captures!) all too well rap's multileveled superiority to late-'70s Punk. A synecdoche is a Part so powerful symbolically as to be eligible for the conceptual absorption, containment, and representation of what it's Part of. A stereotype—immigrant Irish are butt-ugly dumb drunks; poor urban blacks are vulgar and lawless—is just a false synecdoche, a token of the conceptualizer's ignorance or laziness, not of some certain distorted features' representative power. See, though, that, ideologically, genuine Punk was really no different from outside listeners' *stereotype* of Punk. 'Alienated' from everyone and everything, especially itself, Punk couldn't 'speak for' anyone, because Punk couldn't aspire even to the role of Part—'Part' of *what?* There was no

Whole to be Part of in Punk's fashioned, fragmented nihilism, its studied alienation from all 'Wholes' (they even found sex nauseous). The Punks' 'Whole' was themselves, but not as a unit, or even a sum; it was just each of them, individually; together they composed more a sick body's symptom than a functioning digit or limb.

Synecdoche's potency in art depends on a community as backdrop and context, audience, and referent: a definable world for the powerful, dual-functioning Part both to belong to and to transcend.

And this community—slaves, fascists, beats, yippies, B-boys—requires compression by a real (or fancied) Threatening Other outside, in order to reach critical expressive mass.[12] And the circle closeth; for this, too, works both ways. For Us, the bland masses outside its context, the music-of-Others that is rap is easily marginalized through simplification and stereotype into the univocal expression of a single 'subculture' or 'underclass,' one that the media-We have learned to reduce to our own associative stereotypes—poverty, drugs, welfare, obscenity, gangs, entertainment, athletics, teen pregnancy, maleducation…and most of all crime, crime violent and mostly a priori senseless, like some frantic attempt at sign language in the dark; and We talk publicly like We haven't noticed it's been going on this way 10+ years and that the worst of it's always black on black.

Only present and natural, then, that in music as in living we notice by not noticing, by filtering and classifying individual live into social 'Problems' and 'Crises' and 'Wars-On.' Of the 513 art cles on rap/hip-hop indexed in the May '89 *CD ROM* Data Ba only about a third are reviews or critiques of individual recor

---

[12]Public Enemy's first album, *Yo! Bum Rush the Show,* has 'THE GOVERNMENT'S RE SIBLE THE GOVERNMENT'S RESPONSIBLE THE GOVERNMENT'S RESPONSIBLE THE GO MENT'S…' encircling the record's jacket like a Christmas ribbon, or a life pres

and fewer than a dozen pieces are critical attempts to come to terms with the music itself. The rest gather themselves under headlines about the connection between rap and gangs, rap and rape, rap and crack, rap and 'lost generations' We'd never 'found' to begin with. An Entitlement thesis of this whole sampler is simply that critics and writers so far have done a shitty job of countenancing the decade's most important and influential pop movement as anything more than a slide under socio-penology's inverted 'scope.

See that this mainstream attitude is part of yet another loop reinforcing rap's closure and pregnant isolation. Serious rappers seem actually to like—at least they certainly *use*—the following: to judge by what's written and *Donahue*'d by the mainstream, as a cultural force and mass phenomenon the black-music-of-now cannot be understood or even really *heard* by the white-pop-audience-of-now.[13]

t's way too easy for the pale to hurry across the deck, past the thick, ht-wobbling window, and not once hear rap as anything but the rd anthemic march of one Other'd nation, marginalized and yet ɔed in our own metropolitan center, a nation that cannot secede ɪay not assimilate and is thus driven still deeper inside, evincthe brute anger and resentment we'd legitimate as political ɪot anger with nothing visible else to it, no positive diode, ɪe King-like 'vision' we've come to expect from any change ot yield rubble. As an ever more conservative body politic audience, We are being conditioned, in an equation of ɪides may be unconscious, to see today's urban black

the *Voice* puts it better: 'Those whites who felt they were being ɪing" [in rap] had never before encountered the exotic experiɪ pushed into their faces through a hole in the social deck ɪe Race Thing," *Village Voice*, 22 June '89, p. 76.

world not as a demimonde shadowing but more and more as a cancer metastasizing inside our own, our few glimpses of anything like a 'real black world' coming just in statistics and mix radio and political shibboleths—and let's not forget that plucky Jesse Jackson in his bloodstained shirt the AM after King was shot, or the simply outrageous Eddie and Arsenio—or, by the way, that odd graffiti'd window into a cultural explosion whose penumbra leaks out around the intercorporate lens of fashion, soft news, market. Rap/hip-hop is that explosion's leading line of force, that Other nation inside's own personal various Voice, a form of expression scary enough to bind crowds together and drive them. Interested whites, in fortunate or unavoidable moments, can only stare through a window whose bulletproof glass reveals what makes us glad that glass is there. Hell hath no illogic like fear that makes us pay to feel it.

Take the subway farther than usual and see the fear played out at a distance. Dennis Hopper commissions high-priced serious raps for the soundtrack of his '88 *Colors,* a much-acclaimed 'realistic' film that dramatizes gang life in south-central L.A.... except it does so exclusively from the point of view of the white cops assigned to War On it. Real white Boston cops illegally confiscate N.W.A raps about what assholes white cops are. In some big cities it's now S.O.P. for police to pull over and search any black-driven car from which strains of N.W.A issue. A wee-houred college-radio rap show in Cambridge is forced off the air because -bangers keep showing up at the station demanding certain 'requests.'

Or a late-spring Slick Rick concert held in the tiny crowded uncooled gym of Roxbury's Madison Park High. Yr. staff had delicious trouble getting up the nerve even to go, at first. 'Knowledgeable' white friends said we'd be nuts to try. They said our dates would be gang-raped while we were forced to watch and then we'd all be killed amid gales of sinister laughter. Epic anecdotes about black ferocity in Roxbury were related. We listened, read up. We left our dates at home, in their paisley skirts. Decided to dress mean—fatigues, old sneakers, bowling shirts only half-buttoned. Didn't shave. We were scared, but we liked it, the 'danger' involved in just liking rap, from outside. Talk about music with an *edge*. . . .

. . . Well except most of it turned out to be lame hype, these shivered images we'd all formed reading about rap and posses, listening to Ice T's war raps, Public Enemy's prolegomena to any future uprising. At least it turned out to be mostly hype in sinister Roxbury. The ugliest moods at this concert belonged to the 100+ cops in full SWAT regalia—their cars and cycles on full lights, their horses tall and champing in the street outside the high school, the school itself an ugly tumble of slabs that looked like a Fritz Lang set—& to the burly security department that searched (intimately) everyone entering the hot mobbed gym, & to the countless additional 'undercover' (but polyestered, and white) cops inside, heavily armed and sweat-soaked as they prowled the full-court dance floor at time-and-a-half, searching for evidence of those second and third results of the state-of-the-art white autopsy on black community and culture—gangs and 'base cocaine. Evidently the cops had read the same stuff about rap that we had. They and we were suffering a kind of delicious enforced paranoia. The worst violence inflicted that night was on the audience itself: kids, dressed to the eights in white cotton and whisper-thin flats, cramped and hot and to our minds unhumanly patient as they danced and waited for better than three hours of canned or local rap for 'security arrangements' to be nailed down sufficiently to let Slick Rick out of his cream-colored limo and into the arena. The audience put up with the wait, the airless heat, the inadequate facilities, and the cops with a kind of absent amusement; clearly they'd not read or heard what we had, didn't know their script. For the only mediating image between them and the rap Scene was the one the Scene itself projected. They were born inside it, bought in by right, needed no lens or text to see past the 'distance' and 'perspective' administrators and police and sample staff needed to bring to bear.

And but you can feel this false 'perspective,' these lambent, tourist-bringing-his-own-water attitudes in the established rock critics who determine all pop's seriousness, worth, implication— post-hip white staffers of *Stone, Time, Times, Spin.* Often a fatherly condescension about the 'formal novelty' of a genre 'with plenty of energy but not one original sound.' Or sometimes the total acceptance distance breeds, less a criticism than an amused travelogue description, the verbal equivalent of the commuter who'll smile at whatever the bum in his train car says or does just so long as it's not to *him.* But most often a mix of sociological 'objectivity' and extreme personal discomfort, a voice for the white mainstream's fear of (*'concern* over ...,' '*disquiet* about ...,' '*utter lack of pleasure* in listening over and over to ...'[14]) lyrics about crack-smoking, misogyny and rape, shooting and shooting up, Elijah and Malcolm and L. Farrakhan, cop-killing, drive-bys, a nightmarish consumerism manqué, unwillingness to pay dues or sign on the dotted.

Does this concern over a pop's social implications, the relation between a music's and its audience's values, represent something critically new? Elvis got boycotted in the '50s for promoting lewdness and negritude. Cops cruised sock hops. 'Rock 'n' Roll,' after all, meant fucking, and the whole new relation to one's own and partner's bodies spelled sexual frenzy, moral decay, *primitivism.* Might

---

[14]*New York Times,* 28 May 1989, "A&E," pp. 8, 31.

seem Neanderthal now, but at least conservative diatribes against
Elvis were up-front. Today's establishment reviews of rap-as-genre
seem distinguished for the corporate white axioms they assume and
impose on the very music they're remanding to marginal status.
The indictment of rap's 'vague threat,' its connection to the urban-
crisis stats that make us grimace over our morning croissants,
depend especially on a never named, undebated assumption: a pop
art form at once tightly bound up and hugely popular with a certain
social group (or class, or subclass, or subculture) apparently has
Mesmeresque power over it, can not only express or even encourage
but actually dictate attitudes and behavior; can literally *move* its dev-
otees...All subsequent 'critical' questions, then, divide neatly into
what art and where movement. Little hope, for established/-ment
critics, that that movement's toward someplace even roughly parallel to where Yuppie America—the guys with the wallets, the critics'
actual leadership—wants to be. Rap after all is an art form where
shit and *motherfucker* and *pussy* are little more than tics or punctua-
tion. A music in which 'the rhythmic scratching of records [by the
DJ] is a ritualized mutilation of technology, and the spare, clattering
beat propelling so many records bears an unmistakable resemblance to the sound of gunfire.'[15] A pop movement whose thematics
flout mass-music conventions almost DNA-encoded by now, presenting not only themes of what's worst in the world of the postmodern ghetto but presenting them *as* themes, doing so self-consciously,
embodying the Kekulian loop that's now so thoroughly an emblem
of the pop culture rap needs and dismisses, presenting DrugsViolenceGreedDespair as an artistic choice that is *itself* a synecdoche of
decisions about how to live...yes not only relentlessly and self-

---

[15]*New York Times*, 21 May 1989, "A&E," p. 24.

consciously presents but *glorifies*[16] the themes, *romanticizes*[17] them, influences, nay, *exhorts*[18] its audience to understand, respond to, maybe even *embody* certain worsts of those themes....

...So a conservative twist on the old violent-TV-begets-real-violence argument, here. Viz., (TV Violence → Real Violence) as (Porn → Rape) as (Rape → DrugsViolenceGreedDespair) as (Advertising → Consumption). An equation whose only variable is audience. That seems de facto to assume that populations conspicuously susceptible to artistic suggestion are somehow 'childlike.'

But this sort of argument, especially if used by the conservative mainstream, needs to take gauge not just of the responses but also of the inclinations and *predispositions* of the young black urban audience that first granted rap music its Voice. Even powerful art can move only what's moveable; and only a potential——er can actually commit a——, no matter how exhorted. The thing is, what if the Hard rappers' lamest, shallowest responses to their critics are valid: what if the artists are not influencing or informing, but rather just *reflecting* their audience, holding up the mirror their world can see itself as world in? What if they're 'exhorting' B-boys no more than the spectator at a race 'exhorts' the runners?

We suspect here's the root and hidden white mainstream fear: what if cutting-edge rap really *is* a closed music? not even pretending it's promulgating anything controversial or even unfamiliar to its young mass audience? What if rap scares us because it's really just preaching to the converted?

---

[16]*O.E.D.:* 'sings of'
[17]*O.E.D.:* 'versifies'
[18]*O.E.D.:* 'sings to'

D.
(1C)

BASICALLY WE DECIDED we were into rap because, even media hype aside, this music had some kind of hard edge to it. Circa of composition here is July '89. Think back. These last have been fiscal years in which Madonna's 'back on top,' in which covers of classic covers of classic tunes are themselves covered and then climb corporate charts, in which Rod Stewart's out of cryogenics and back on top....MTV's ceased to be anything but a long commercial for itself and the interests of corporate labels; Bobby McFerrin makes a platinum mint and then several commercial jingles out of a burbled synth-reggae invitation to "Be Happy," a song that has the same verbal prepackaging feel as 'Where's the Beef?' and 'You Look Mahvlus' and other linguistic equivalents of the Pet Rock....Last year heavy metal's fake-Satanist male models accounted for ½ of total US record sales; U2 filmed a $20,000,000 homage to their own self-righteousness and Bono's ever less well-disguised megalo-mania. A year when even good old REM finally went corporate pop with *Green,* when good old Springsteen trashed his bride, when as modest and nascent a talent as Tracy Chapman earned cymbal-crashing critical raves for her competent, updated frappé of Baez and Armatrading, so desperate were pop critics and consumers for any voice at once comprehensible and even remotely fresh, sincere, musical via *something to say.* Desperate for any kind of edge we can get ourselves to *feel,* it seems like. Just not notable pop years at all. Except in rap. Rap appears in the famished late '80s as potentially a genuine musical Scene the way early jazz, rock, the Summer of Love, folk/protest, god even the way New Wave and Punk were 'Scenes'—the S-word here simultaneously meaning: something new to look at; something loud and upsetting ('Oh please, Veronica, let's not have a *Scene!*'); and, best, an identifiable set of places-in-time where large forces meet, marry, and beget. Whether by virtue or default, rap is pretty much what there is to like, right now, if you want to regard today's pop as anything more than covert jingles in $^4/_4$ time. In our opinion.

But so the point is we enjoy it. Plus we've developed some theses about why serious rap is important, both as art-for-own-sake and as a kind of metaphor-with-larynx for a subbed-culture unique in its distillation of the energy and horror of the urban American present.

Plus our attempts at this sampler have yielded for us the belief—which this'll be all about defending—that '89–'90 rap, for all its bombed-out cynicism, hermeticism, hostility, and crudeness, should also be an important music—important in different ways explainable by parallax—both *to* and *for* a young white American mainstream dammed up by the very bed it's made itself to flow in.

Hence the decision that this sampler-from-outside is worth the trouble of actually writing out…plus it gets to be didactic, which one of us loves. Plus the prenominate fact that so very little has been well-written about serious rap/hip-hop and attendant phenomena, except for Concerned Editorial Handwringing at the movement as nothing less than the first fray in a social fabric's rending, at the serious crews and cuts themselves as just the flashy communiqués of a culture we're at 'War-On' with. So basically virgin territory, to essay into. Ecological niche to fill. Viable Gap in Market. What better entitlements than these? For they segue so nicely into the really salient, rap-esque rationale: we get to because we want to. The headlong pursuit of present-tense pleasure, after all, has risen to chief among American rights; no? And since a whole main-stream's pretty much decided what it wants to need, apparently, the biggest challenge is just the new old one: how to get you to buy.

2. IMPEDIMENT

D.
(2A)

BECAUSE WE'RE ADMITTING up-front it's an unlikely product. Even of sampling. It's like Get Out of Their Church on Sunday: whatever musical or sociopolitical importances there are in rap/hip-hop are pretty obviously there to be drawn out by and for black people.[1] The fenestrated barriers to any real upscale white appreciation of rap and its Scene looked almost Romanesque-esque until we hit on the The-Barriers-Are-*Part*-of-Any-White-Appreciation strategy, the one that yielded Entitlement.

But plus age issues. While many of the top rap performers are of

---

[1] Cf. 'The Sultan,' editor of *The Source*, a new kind of *Tiger Beat* of rap:

> It took Public Enemy to make us realize that we can fight back, that we don't have to accept *their* guidelines for how to interpret *our* music.

majority, the mass of their audience is not. At the Slick Rick affair this May, M. observed grimly that he didn't know whether he felt more isolated by color or by age. We're a well-preserved 26. We do not generate gaps. Still, I kept having this disturbing vision of like Hugh Beaumont and Robert Young at a Hendrix show. And the real rap concert scene, like the music itself, is shut tight against white faces. The Madison Park High audience who turned out to see the Returning Ruler, as mentioned above, didn't hassle or abuse us. Actually it was worse. They acted like we weren't there. Eye contact was impossible: they'd focus on whatever was behind us. People ran into us with neither hostility nor apology. Remember Richard Pryor had this great routine about how when he went to Africa he knew for the very first time what it must feel like to be white in America? This scene was the neat obverse. We didn't even qualify as interlopers: we were so conspicuous we were invisible. And we were weirdly disappointed. We'd bagged our dates, dressed mean, gotten all ready for Trouble in Art's Name. We were used to *existing*, dammit. We did manage to get our car's tire slashed for Art, but that means only that they noticed our white Pinto. Or maybe not: the slashers got the whole parking lot.

And impediment-wise downhill even from there, for a while. Hanging inconspicuously out, à la McPhee, was impossible: at least McPhee's subjects acknowledge his presence. People in the Boston, New York, L.A., Chicago, Washington, Minneapolis, and St. Louis rap Scenes (yr. staff knocked at all seven doors) were just not into fresh white unfamiliar faces. Clubs tended to be so loud you couldn't ask anybody anything. Expert sources, like local DJs and rappers—even just a likely-looking -banger with a big tape player on his shoulder—when approached by a scrubbed white male (who, though dressed mean, might very well be a cleverly disguised yuppie trendhorse) with questions about This Whole Nutty Confusing Rap

Scene, invariably do one of two things. One is that they'll look you up coldly from loafers to eyes and then turn very deliberately to look somewhere else. It's a 'dis.' If the person's a girl and has other girls with her she will often say something unintelligible to them that makes them all laugh so hard their hands go to their mouths. Or two is that the 'expert source' will smile broadly and seem friendly and maybe helpful, but you notice he's wearing sunglasses indoors, and it turns out he'll answer only very specific questions, so specific they require 'yes' or 'no,' without one skein of help regarding how one might get, interrogatively, to the specific. And the few 'into it' white fans around the rap penumbra tended to babble and pester the essayist for drugs and were no help and could not give consistent answers even to the question of where they were. Efforts at interviewing rap producers involved *scores* of messages left on answering machines as far west as St. Louis and as far south as Savannah, GA, our personal favorite machine belonging to Roxbury's own Ocean Records, whose recorded message intones occultly over dub-reggae

THE HOUR OF THE RETURN

IS UPON US.

Please leave a message at the beep.[2]

---

[2]Although we know of no music actually produced by Ocean Records, its phone machine's message is a small masterpiece of menace and mystery. Check it out late some night at 617-787-0457. Note that for non-Bostonians THIS IS A TOLL CALL— make sure to check w/ Mom and Dad before dialing. For potential future presidential appointees: do NOT leave your name, since Ocean Records has got to be on some kind of FBI wiretap list, and who needs a Senator in 1999 bringing up goofy phone messages left on a Jamaican drug kingpin's front company's machine back in 1990?

Don't worry about an actual human being answering at Ocean Records; this has never happened to us in some four months of prank calling. — M.

... The RETURN in question was never a returned phone call, apparently, since our overtures to everyone met with utter blankness until the brothers Smith cracked the door a little and gave us a peek at North Dorchester's RJam.

Our ironic fortune, it finally turned out, was the fact that rap is just not a scene much into 'literary essays,' not really a clue about what they even are, until the 'essayist' explains he's like a reporter who gets to talk for a really long time. It occurred lightbulb-like to yr. staff that here *They* were irrevocably outside *Our* scene, complete woods-babes when it came to the violent & debased world of creative writing / criticism; had not even a vision of such a world... *except thru the window of pop/media stereotype.* And this window turned out to be the one of our opportunity.

For of course it meant that, using the only fail-safe cultural carapace of the late '80s, reliable old self-parody, we could simply assume the 2-D identities of the stereotypical 'Intellectual/Writer,' *be* the way an alien, whose lone access was pop representation, might see us. Thespian requirements here included: turtlenecks; gleaming unwashed hair, the thickest spectacles on the clear-lens rack; leather patches at tweed elbows, maybe a modest brier; and a manner combining the nerdy earnestness of *Gilligan's Isle*'s Professor with the abashed '70s liberalism of whites on *Maude, Jeffersons, Good Times,* and so on.

Thus we huddled. Mutually exhorted. Got psyched down. Dressed unmean. Exfoliated all pride in advance. Shed dignity in sheets until we had no style, no 'play,' no face at all. In other words we finally came on like such overwhite ephebes, such complete fools, that making fools of us just wasn't worth anybody's energy. Eureka, etc. For lo a precious couple of those in-Scene began responding, treating our inquiries as a polite adult would the questions of a child whose list he can only hope is finite.

For instance did you know it turns out this 'new music' isn't even music? Music is 'the art of organizing tones to produce a coherent sequence of sounds intended to elicit an aesthetic response from the listener,' or 'vocal or instrumental sounds having some degree of rhythm, melody and harmony.'[3] Even on the casualest surface, rap is a genre without harmonics or counterpoint. And the response it's aiming to elicit is to aesthetics what maybe a demo derby is to a Vermeer. And there's not really melody here, even, unless one counts a bass rhythm in $^4/_4$ cut time repeated over and over in a near-parodic *ostinato* until its own dense stasis starts to sound weirdly like movement, development, the most tightly bound sound sequence imaginable. The only bona fide 'music' in rap issues from computerized matrices, hand-scratched records, and digitally manipulated samples of other people's music...plus of course the rhymes of the rapper, and often the ad-lib of his call's responder, the DJ(-s): Terminator X and Flavor Flav of Public Enemy, Salt's Pepa, DJ Jazzy Jeff, Eazy-E and MC Ren of N.W.A. Though, to be scrupulous about what's music, everyone with ears has gleaned by now that the vocals in rap (unless they're sampled snatches) are never tonal or modulated: they're recited, declaimed, or most often just yelled, unsweetened by any crossover from shout's pitch to song's note.

Which is of course just to say that this isn't the *O.E.D.*'s — that bible of educated expectation's — 'music,' this weird shit. Its values and foci are different, its precedents un-Anglo. Like the drum machine and scratch, sample and backbeat, the rapper's 'song' is essentially an upper layer in the dense weave of *rhythm* that, in rap, usurps melody and harmony's essential functions of identification,

---

[3] *O.E.D.*: defs. 1 & 2.

call, counterpoint, movement, and progression, the play of woven notes...until 'rhythm' comprises the essential definitions of rap itself: dance beats that afford unlimited bodily possibility, married rhythmically to complexly stressed lyrics that assert, both in message and meter, that things now can never be other than what *IS*. It's the contrapuntal tension between the music's celebration of freedom-in-Space (dance) and the rap's tightly rhymed and metered rhetoric of imprisonment-in-Time, of a poverty of 'set' and self that allows only status and power as value and only neighborhood as audience...it's this tension that gives rap's 'talk-on records' their special and poignantly post-Reagan edge.

M.
(2B)

Free Sample 1

FOR OUTSIDERS, RAP'S hard to dissect, easy to move to. The command is: dance, don't understand; participate, don't manipulate. Rap is a fortress protected by twin moats of talk and technology. The first is a nu style of speak—the 'dialect drug' De La Soul calls it—that rappers fashion from jive and disseminate through record stores to all of us. Some in-words, like 'fly,' meaning 'fine-looking,' have been in coin since the beginning, now venerable as Old English because they turn up on Grandmaster Flash cuts from '82. Others, like 'dead presidents,' rap for $, are either coming into or going out of currency, depending on when you read this. Rap, a club language, has myriad ways to describe one's own or others' looks. 'Fly' is how a man digs a woman. One would never describe oneself as 'fly,' even when cataloguing one's own attractions (done more in rap than anyplace except perhaps *Village Voice* personals). 'Fresh' means irresistibly stylish, oft-modified by 'funky,' 'crazy,' or 'stoopid,' predominantly used to convey the fly-ness of things other than women, including oneself or one's rap, which two concepts rappers, like schizophrenics, can't always keep separate in their heads. 'Dope' means 'def,' and 'def' means crazy funky *stoopid* fresh. Synonyms include: the shit, the It, the cool, the thang, the word, the grooviest, the categorical imperative, *die Weltanschauung,* the that-which-Potter-Stewart-would-know-if-he-saw. A def rapper is so style-defining as to make the stylish mere copycats. To be def is to rap to the beat of a different drum machine — not seeking solitude, but rather confident that others will follow. The def rapper MC's a def rap, which rap def-ly tells of its own (and the rapper's) def-ness — so def, as MC/manager/entrepreneur Russell Rush Simmons brags, that it had to be on a label called Def Jam.

Rap celebrates power, equating strength with style, and style with the 'I' in 'Individuality.' Rappers 'dis' — dis-miss — the style-less, faceless. To 'ill' is to be weak or wrong; to 'bite' is to thieve another's dope beat. And only the ill would bite.

But here's the paradox out of which this sampler grows: def raps are only those bitten so def-ly as to cancel the source. In rap, existence is erection. The opposite of def is death. And the best proof of a right to use the phallic pronoun is to be so stylishly you that others (try to) dis or bite you, but cannot — repeat: *cannot* — ignore you. Fine, except that 99% of all serious rap, from platinum-selling Public Enemy to North Dorchester's Tam-Tam, is built on 'sampling,' a term taken from high-tech rather than jive, latest in a train of studio remastering advances that began in the 'sound factories' of '60s wizard producers like Andrew Loog Oldham, George Martin, and Phil Spector. When Elvis cut "Hound Dog" in '58, he and his band did something like 51 takes, simply because, with five performers and no mixing, 51 takes were needed for all five to get it right on the same take. Recording without mixing is simply live music saved for later. Mixing, the mortar in Phil Spector's infamous "Wall of Sound," allowed a track to feature one artist playing several instruments, or harmonizing with himself, or merging his own work with other recorded music or noise. Take two tape recorders: Elvis could sing lead vocals on Tape 1, play that tape back, and harmonize with his own recorded voice while Tape 2 picked up the result.

Early remastered pop was the first fake music ever, since what the record buyer of '63 experienced as Aural Event on his turntable couldn't happen live. Rock began to become an Illusion of Event that technology made possible; rock became more like the movies, starting down a long road at the end of which was MTV.

Not that this is what kept Phil Spector up nights. The gurus of the studio had fatter fish to clean, for the new freedom to shape sound had come at a price. With each magnetic jump from live, as tape was made of tapes that were themselves tapes of tapes, the hiss and crackle of interference multiplied. Dual high-bias media with 2 units each of sonic garbage per 10,000 units of Elvis Presley, retaped on similar 2-units-per-10,000 tape, became 4 units of hiss; retaped, 8; then 16; then 32. As the sound got fuller, it decayed.

The solution was a breakthrough called multitracking—using recorders that could capture and play back on 2 (as in stereo), 4 (as in '67's then-ear-shattering *Sgt. Pepper's Lonely Hearts Club Band*), 12, 16, and today 24 parallel tracks, eliminating the hiss of transference from one machine to the next. Rhythms, melodies, harmonies, could all be captured on separate tracks, allowing the performer or producer to mix and listen and remix, adding vocals or lead instrument on yet another track. Rap Edisons like Kool Herc, Grandmaster Flash, and Afrika Bambaataa began as party DJs, not musicians.

Their wiring of twin turntables to a mixer, allowing them to 'stack' the sound of two different records while rapping into a mike, was a kind of crude, extemporaneous multitracking. Technological loops like those in the NASA-esque studios of CBS and Polygram were now in the hands of the homeboys. Carter was President. The Bee Gees, with five Top 10 hits in 12 months, were king.

Digital recording, the science dividing RJam's Tam-Tam on tape from Tam-Tam as heard 'live,' is a technology that converts music to codes, or 'digits.' The codes are 'read' by a computer, one combining sophisticated sound-to-code translation hardware with a number-crunching COS and a high-response synthesizer, at speeds of 40,000 digits per second and up. The recorded sounds, reduced to numbers, can be shaped, mangled, muffled, amplified, and even canonized.[1] Hardware then translates the digits, as read and altered, back into sound, which can itself be recorded on multi-track and combined with yet more sounds. The result: hiss-free reproduction on an infinity of tracks, each of which tracks can itself be manipulated infinitely.

Digital recording, part of the '80s sea change in how pop gets made, divides the responsibility for the final 'song' more or less equally among the performer, the engineer at the mixing board, the producer who coordinates the multitracking and mixing process, and the electronic hardware that actually 'makes' the music we buy. The latest synthesizers[2] produce notes from pure electric

---

[1] 'Canon' being another non-jive rap term, meaning the division of a single sequence of sound into two or more repeating sound sequences, like a vocal round.

[2] ...themselves the heirs of a long 20th-century evolutionary process, from the player-piano to the '20s' ondes Martenot and Theremin and Trautonium (crude electronic instruments big in France), to Pierre Schaeffer's *musique concrète* in 1948, to the first Electronic Music Synthesizer invented by engineers at RCA in the '50s, to

current instead of electronically amplified vibrations, with voltage meters rather than hands or feet determining everything from key to pitch to timbre to 'attack-delay envelope' (another non-rap term, denoting the microtimed, counterpoised quality of a note's duration, how a note's sound/quaver-structure as it builds is different from its sound and structure as it fades—the manipulation of a piano's foot pedals, for example, affects the delay component of each note and chord's envelope). The Kurzweil 250, a state-of-the-art system, is a 12-track/12,018-note synthesizer linked by software to an Apple Macintosh Plus, which serves as an exhaustive library of digitized sound. The Kurzweil could put all of culture in a blender—take Janet Leigh's Cremora-curdling scream from *Psycho,* store it in the Mac, program the synth such that an F# will be reproduced as Janet Leigh's F# scream, then play "We Shall Overcome" as if screamed by Janet Leigh; store this; treat similarly Bach's *St. Matthew Passion,* except with vast choruses of screaming Janet Leighs, then "Mary Had a Little Lamb," then "Twist and Shout" (the Isleys', not the Beatles'), all as screams; then replay the four as one horrific jumble, or select amidst the jumble; and then whatever you came up with in the final, painstakingly remixed mix you could play backward. And call that 'finished.' Or never finish. It's like holding music at gunpoint. You can make it do—or do to you—whatever you can think of. Whim is the only limit.

And the sound? A comparatively crude digital process yields

---

the inauguration of the Columbia-Princeton Electronic Music Center in 1959, to Robert Moog's 1964 development of the Moog 55, the first emitter of amplified 'blurps, fwipps, simps, twings, and schlonks' to be commercially produceable. Walter/Wendy Carlos used a Moog 55 for his/her 1968 *Switched-On Bach,* an album that did more than anything to popularize synthesized sound. —D.

immaculate CDs, beside which vinyl records and magnetized cassettes sound like hasty wiretaps.

Technical definitions notwithstanding, 'sampling' the music of others did not begin with digital multitracking any more than travel began with Apollo 7. DJ Jazzy Jeff's re-use of the *I Dream of Jeannie* theme is but one theft in a hoary history of 'musical quotation' going back to Bach—who ripped off 17th-century court dances in his *French Suites*—and before. Contemporary experimental art-music composers like Glass, Reich, Cage, Chatham, Eno, and Van Tieghem assemble 'sound collages' out of random bits of everyday noise. These modern composers 'vandalize' the tradition of classicism by forcing that tradition to swallow plain old noise within the classically developed musical genres of suite, symphony, sonata, even opera.

Rap, like the avant-garde, deploys digital multitracked sampling to blow open the musical and political boundaries of the soul and funk that are the rappers' Bach and Beethoven. Public Enemy's *Yo! Bum Rush the Show* and *It Takes a Nation of Millions to Hold Us Back*, cruising at 100–120 beats/minute, weave thick 'sound carpets' of tempo, other tempo, guitar riffs, constant sirens, radio tunings, buzz saws (or is that a dentist's drill on P.E.'s "Terminator X Speaks With His Hands"?), motors, weird noises, chatter, and rhyme. P.E.'s producers, Hank Shocklee and Carl Ryder, wield techniques invented to eliminate sonic garbage to *enhance* that garbage. The result: aural paranoia.

> *Go, go, go, go, go, go*
> *Take a look at his style*
> *Take a check of the sound*
> *Off the record, people keeping him down*

Trick a chick in Miami
Terminator X packs the jams

…Chuck D rants on "Terminator X to the Edge of Panic," a tribute to Terminator X, his sample-scratching sidekick. But Chuck's delivery abolishes verses, leaving no listening space between either his beats or his words. He tells you to go go go, but won't let you out.

In fact, *Smoke Some Kill* and *Nation of Millions* are part of rap's 'Coming of Age,' which a *Los Angeles Times* feature story hailed February '89.[3] This move is, in part, a diversification into topics well beyond the simple get-off-my-basketball-court formulas so dear to pioneers like Sugarhill Gang and Grandmaster Flash. Rap's world is widening, taking in Leviticus, AIDS, famine, the Oliver North trial, all that pop and folk have ever taken in and more, with sampling as the side door. Schoolly D proclaims his militant pride in color, sampling a speech by cop-slain Black Panther H. Rap Brown in "Black Man," making pride into an overtly political text. L.A.'s posse 7A3 chant, 'It's a mad, mad world,' sampling as evidence actual news broadcasts of gang shootings, police brutality, and plane crashes. Stetsasonic enjoyed a black-chart hit in '88 with "A.F.R.I.C.A.," an anti-apartheid cut in the "We Are the World" tradition, featuring a digital mix of Jesse Jackson and African percussionist Babatunde Olatunji.

Sampling is also the source of the freaky slapstick, witting and otherwise, that is rap's other half. Mr. Ed's immortal 'Hullo, Wilbur' has turned up several times, the intro to *The Bugs Bunny Hour,* so far, only once. And some of the freest, funniest use of sampling comes from the new decade's hottest crew, De La Soul, who begin

---

[3] 21 February 1989, p. D 2.

their "Plug Tunin'" with a '30s radio announcer's plucky yet worried 'Good luck to both of you!' as if our hip-hop heroes were attempting a cross-Channel swim. Other cuts on *3 Feet High and Rising* feature a '50s crooner slowed to a slur, Liberace canonized till he sounds like a creepy hypnotist, repetitive loops of an elementary French lesson...and the record's intro is a manic parody host of MTV's own game-show parody, *Remote Control,* asking whether we, as contestants/listeners, are ready to 'play the game.'

The game has stakes. DJ Jazzy Jeff and the Fresh Prince build their "Girls Ain't Nothing But Trouble" rap around the title tinkle from *I Dream of Jeannie,* forty-nine seconds of brainless pseudo-Bedouin schlock that was, for many of us, a beloved fixture each day in reruns. "Girls Ain't Nothing But Trouble" is itself quintessential Fresh Prince, the title spelling out his very profoundest conclusions on the matter, as told through examples of times in the day-to-day life of the Unspoiled Heir when, yes, a particular girl turned out to be nuttin but trouble. It's a song-genre white sources have been working since the beginning (remember "It's My Party and I'll Cry If I Want To" or "Teen Angel"?), but it jars to hear it from two tall black men in denim, gold, and leather hats. It's as if Public Enemy sampled Louis Farrakhan on "The White Capitalist Oligarchy Ain't Nothing But Trouble," complaining

> *The white systum*
> *Is a pain in my bum.*

We are tempted to imagine even wilder crossover failures: James Brown, Godfather of Soul, singing the part of Ivnglg, some Nordic war god straight outta Wagner's *Ring* cycle, or Neil Sedaka in leather warm-ups covering K-9 Posse's "This Beat Is Military," singing

Callin' strikes of the air
Declarin' aerial warfare.

But the one non-mediocre thing in "Girls Ain't Nothing But Trouble" is utter rap genius: DJ Jazzy Jeff's bold theft of the almost psychedelically out-of-place *I Dream of Jeannie* theme. It is, after all, one thing to steal a car, quite another to steal the daisy-painted prop the clowns drive under the big top. And, yes, as the Fresh Prince bitches on about da bitches, we find ourselves warming to the idea of a brand-new, heretofore unthought-of *I Dream of Jeannie:* a '60s sitcom with rappers. It's a fun, and funny, idea; and the humor is the uneasy pleasure we would have if *I Dream of Jeannie* episodes ended somehow differently in '90s rerun than they did in '70s rerun, if we tuned in one day in the early months of the Bush administration to find hippies camping on *Bonanza,* lesbians leaving it to Beaver, and, yes, chain-wearing B-boys checking out Jeannie's butt and bare midriff as she attempts to fathom the mysteries of supermarket shopping. Many would be outraged, as if the boob tube broke its word. Suddenly, watching *I Dream of Jeannie* is as risky as life itself; suddenly you don't know at exactly what moment Roger Healey will interrupt, asking, 'Am I interrupting?' — in fact for once you don't know whether he'll interrupt at all, or be in this episode, or what this episode will be about. You started the half hour with the *I Dream of Jeannie* that predates puberty, a show you've dug longer than you've dug girls (and expect to still dig in the old folks' home when the girl fad has passed). But *then,* without warning, Jazzy Jeff and the Fresh Prince show up in Tony Nelson's Cocoa Beach, asking Jeannie if she's got plans for the rest of the afternoon. It'd seem surreally unjust, like being asked to do puberty again at 26.

Couldn't happen, of course, because every American knows that the first shit-talking black on TV was Sherman Hemsley's George Jefferson on *All in the Family,* five or six years later, which is just another way of saying that the '60s sitcom was a white playground, a Rhodesian cricket-test of the brain, whose segregation was enforced only by the floating rules of genre. It's not that shit-talking blacks were barred from shows like *Bewitched* and *The Munsters,* or that plots obviously calling for blacksploitation films' ill-tempered Jim Brown were cast instead with Tom Bosley; rather, blacks never made it to the '60s sitcom because . . . what would they do there? The '60s sitcom was an overworld of witches, genies, Martians, ghosts, talking horses, thinking pigs, campy P.O.W. camps, patented mayhem as seemingly ruleless as a drama without genre. But ask yourself: is it more far-fetched that Jim Brown would guest-spot on *I Dream of Jeannie,* or that a show about an astronaut living with a bottled sexpot, one that made no reference to sex, much less racial strife, would rivet America's attention in the summer of '67, when riots erupted in every major city? Which is weirder: an *I Dream of Jeannie* with blacks or without them? Answer: they're equally weird. Yet the second has haunted syndicated airwaves for two decades, while the first would punch a hole in the walls of rerun worlds as familiar to us as the little screen itself.

This division of experience into 'weird' and 'normal,' Them and Us, Terrorist and Freedom Fighter, voodoo and Roman Catholicism, is at the heart of white ambivalence about rap music. Just as N.W.A tell interviewers that their controversially violent *Straight Outta Compton* shocks only those who don't live with violence every day, so *I Dream of Jeannie*'s mix of erotic chastity / magical science could only seem like 'normal' prime-time fare for suburbanites raised on sitcoms. Every travelogue is somebody else's home movie.

Every audience is two: that rapt because it finally hears its stories being told, and that rapt because it finally hears a story so utterly divorced from its own as to seem weird. These two groups — united nowhere else in life — share, in mass popular art, one audienceship, an illusion of union. Jazzy Jeff, wringing laughs from the incongruity of his sampling, rides this audience politics as far as it will go, making *I Dream of Jeannie*, of all things, a rap song — strange to those for whom genie-owning astronauts had become passé — also strange for those inside rap who have *their* notions of what's apposite — and, in its dual strangeness, a funny reunion all over again.

Consider *I Dream of Jeannie*. This prime-time, Mondays-at-8 offering was just plain weird. A sitcom about one man's heroic quest for Hooverian Normalcy. Tony Nelson's the Man of Science from '50s documentaries called *Our Friend the Atom*. His Pandora is a mini–Marilyn Monroe,[4] named by her agent after Paradise. Major Nelson's weekly problem is that reality isn't stable enough. But say 'stable' and Jeannie will get confused and blink Man o' War onto the patio. Later in the episode, his jockey will appear, pissed. In elaborate half hours, tangled confusions about what is or should be real are themselves entanglingly covered up, countenanced, resolved, finally returning us (suburbanites back from a mind vacation) in 30 minutes to the real beginning.

An episode initially aired on June 12, 1967, features Tony, the space-age American, idly wishing aloud that he could live in the Old West, when men were Men. Jeannie, eager, all-powerful, and

---

[4] Literally. Barbara Eden broke in on a short-lived small-screen version of *Gentlemen Prefer Blondes* from '63, with Eden in Marilyn Monroe's film role. Her real last name is Schlajanzky, or something.

literal-minded (a deadly sit-combo), sends him and us back to Gopher Gulch, an old *Rawhide* set terrorized by rustlers led by veteran B-movie cowboy crooner Hoyt Axton. A *High Noon* spoof ensues, with Tony in good-guy white shooting his own foot but refusing Jeannie's help: he must face Hoyt Axton alone. Tony finally 'wins' their burlesque gunfight, and he and Jeannie return to Cocoa Beach with a minute or so left in the episode (like suburbanites back from vacation the night before a workday) and just enough script left to savor, with an interrupting Roger Healey, their ended adventure.

Did anyone on the evening of June 12, 1967, snap off the set as the pseudo-Bedouin closing played to the roll of credits, turn to her hubby, and say, 'What the hell was *that*'? The *High Noon* spoof certainly is a freaky premise for fantasy: Tony's unwanted peril follows from *getting* his wish; but it turns out that this peril, this wish-gone-awry, is what he had craved without knowing it. All in a fantasy Florida never to be confused with the actual Florida of Walter Cronkite, itself the scene of some distinctly unfunny race riots in Tampa, which began the night before Tony Nelson went back to the Old West and raged at their worst between 8 PM and midnight Eastern Time, Monday, June 12, 1967, as the *High Noon* spoof aired.

The Tampa riots began on a muggy Sunday night when the falsely rumored shooting of a black youth by Tampa police brought aimless crowds onto the streets. Fires were started. Cops (who no doubt fantasized, like fellow Floridian Tony Nelson, that they could be cowboys) arrived and shoved a few kids. That's really all it took: liquor and appliance stores were looted along the main drag of Black Tampa, TVs presumably stolen and plugged in, perhaps to NBC's local affiliate, just in time to see Tony Nelson wishing idly aloud that he could return to when men were Men. Mayhem came next. To quote the *Report of the National Advisory Commission on Civil Disorders:*

> Driving along the expressway [near downtown Tampa], a young white couple, Mr. and Mrs. C.D., were startled by the fires. Deciding to investigate, they took the off-ramp into the midst of the riot. The car was swarmed over. Its windows were shattered. [Mr.] C.D. was dragged into the street....J.C., a Negro fruit-picker from Arkansas, was as surprised by the riot as [the young white couple]. Rushing toward the station wagon in which the young woman was trapped, he interposed himself between her and the mob.[5]

A world would end if the mob at the foot of that Tampa off-ramp spilled into the Cocoa Beach of *I Dream of Jeannie.* Not onto the set of the television show, but rather, mystically, into the June 12, 1967, episode *itself,* posing a genre challenge the '60s sitcom never faced: absorb our riot; prove that you're real enough. The NBC writers would brainstorm as the angry mob milled around on Tony Nelson's Cocoa Beach lawn. Panicky calls from network and White House come in every five minutes: 'Have you thought of anything yet?' Tony Nelson would be hastily scripted to handle Hoyt Axton in five minutes instead of 25, then hastily flown by prop to Cocoa Beach to broker an overnight truce between the mob and the all-white Tampa police force, presiding at a Coroner's

---

[5] *Report of the National Advisory Commission on Civil Disorders* (New York: Bantam Books, 1968), pp. 44–45.

Inquest to prove that the rumored shooting that sparked the riots had in reality never happened. Jeannie, eager if inept, would try to help by blinking Martin Luther King (the gracious civil rights leader agreeing to play himself in the interests of ending the violence) from Atlanta to plead for everyone to go back to their homes. King, however, is written to believe that the entire tableau is a product of a covert LSD dosing by the CIA, and tells Jeannie she isn't really real. 'Oh, and I bet you're Tommy Nelson, the famous astronaut,' King says, pointing at Nelson. 'That's *Tony*,' Larry Hagman corrects. (Laughter.)

The network, seeing that King has been scripted to refuse to help on the grounds that none of this is really happening, calls up the writers: 'What the hell are you bastards doing down there? Have King speak to the goddamn rioters!'

But the writers cannot. This is a sitcom, after all, and they can no more violate genre than God can create something more perfect than Himself. There must be a situation that is comedic, and they have resorted to that oldest situation: disbelief. Meanwhile, back within the episode, the Florida National Guard, pelted with rocks and epithets, are fixing bayonets. Tony Nelson orders Jeannie to blink their rifles into cellos. (Laughter.) Malcolm X (portrayed by the versatile Nipsey Russell) is blinked back from Muslim Heaven, which looks suspiciously like the set used for scenes inside Jeannie's bottle; and King and X argue about whose fault these riots (which King still maintains aren't happening) are, until Jeannie intervenes. She pleads sweetly, looking straight at the camera (Barbara Eden *smelling* her first Emmy)

> We must come together. Why can't we come together?
> Come on, why the long faces? [She tickles Malcolm X,

who, in spite of himself, grins.] That's right, Mr. X.
And you, Dr. King? Can't you give us a smile?

If this were an MGM musical, now might be an excellent
moment for Barbara Eden to break into song, leading everybody
(Malcolm X, the Tampa Police Chief, Dr. Bellows) in rings around
the Chryslers in the carport. Instead, the civil rights rivals are
scripted to see the folly of their feud. Uniting, they placate the rioters. Order is restored, and a chastised Tampa Police Chief vows
that in future things will be more just. His attack dog barks in
cheerful agreement, prompting the inevitable sitcom close: 'That
makes it unanimous!' (Uneasy Laughter. Applause.)

Rap's sampling of *I Dream of Jeannie* blends homage and ram-
page, celebrating the open-ended transferability of shared culture
and attacking the segregation of the icon by mock-integrating it.
Another pantomime of desegregation comes from Run-DMC's
"Walk This Way," a monster hit among young whites in '86 that
samples Aerosmith's equally huge '77 hit so extensively that it is
unclear without checking the record jacket who's sampling whom.
The cut's MTV incarnation, surely the most widely seen rap video
ever, flaunts rap's Cain-and-Abel relationship with heavy metal,
itself the 'house music' of Burger Kings in Howard Beach, Queens.

Run-DMC practice in a ratty ghetto back room. Their labors
are disrupted by thunderous metal chords, which we — being a
typical Tuesday-at-3-PM MTV audience — recognize as Aerosmith, a hard-rocking Boston foursome redolent of Pabst-sneaking
on soccer fields a decade ago. Not good memories, but strong ones.

The joke is that in the Burger Kings of Hollis, Queens, Aerosmith is merely bad, unfamiliar noise, and Run-DMC can barely
stand it, making fingers-in-ears gestures to one another, mimicking

for a splendid moment suburban Dads yelling upstairs for Junior to turn down that goddamn stereo. They snap out of Dad mode, however, coming through the busted wall, looking to leave Adidas prints on whoever's responsible. Beyond the wall they find, naturally enough, an Aerosmith stadium extravaganza like those of yore fronted by lead singer Steve Tyler dressed in the same stupid elf-wizard outfit he was wearing last time anyone was paying attention. The rappers menace Tyler, and a sick pleasurable fear rises in our MTV-watching hearts: B-boys have invaded the white side of the '70s, and wouldn't it be a horrible relief to have rap, for once, act out the violence it suggests? Wouldn't we love to hate to see rap kick heavy metal's acne'd ass, swinging guitars (so often, since Elvis, wielded as icons of beatings, as dildo-guns or dildo-axes) to silence the guitarists?

But no, we're teased again. Run-DMC decide they *like* this stuff, and the two groups join unlikely forces. Steve Tyler, who can't dance, teaches everybody how.

Ironies abound, of course, as ironies must when cash and art do lunch. Tearing down the prop-thin symbolic walls, Run-DMC aim to celebrate desegregation, but miss the fact that Aerosmith, those whitest of white rockers, are merely big-budget Led Zeppelin rip-offs, and that Led Zep came straight outta the jet-black Rhythm & Blues of Chicago's Chess Records. Dancing with Steve Tyler, Run-DMC forget that Muddy Waters's sideman Willie Dixon had to *sue* Led Zeppelin to get proper credit for their use of his blues. "Walk This Way" is an unwanted reunion of '80s black street music with part of its rich heritage, as that heritage has been mined and mongrelized by Show Biz. If this is desegregation, then shopping malls hold treasure.

D.
(2C)

STILL, SOMEWHERE ALONG the line something can happen where you think you all of a sudden understand why this weird closed antimusic holds such jittery fascination for you who are outside it, getting the 'Real Thing' mostly off discs and equipment in cozy Boston digs, able to turn the stuff on and off, listening with the blank distant intensity of someone gazing out the window of a fast train.

Do those of you in like Chicago or NYC ever notice how commuters on the train tend to get all quiet and intense when South Side or South Bronx starts to flow past? If you look closely at the faces, you see it's not depression, not even discomfort; it's a kind of rigid fascination with the beauty of ruins in which people live but look or love nothing like you, a horizonful of numbly complex vistas in slab-gray and spraypaint-red. Hieroglyphs on walls, people on stoops, hoops w/o nets. White people have always loved to gaze at the 'real black world,' preferably at a distance and while moving briskly through, toward business. A view from this remove yields easy abstractions about rap in its role as just the latest 'black' music. Like: the less *real* power a people have, the more they'll assert hegemony in areas that don't much matter in any grand scheme. A way to rule in hell: their own vocabulary, syntax, gestures, music, dance; own food; religious rhetoric; social and party customs; that...*well-known* athletic superiority—the foot-speed, vertical leap—we like them in fields, cotton- or ball-.[1] It's a Hell we like to look at because it has so clearly been made someone else's very own....And the exported popular arts! the singing and dancing!...each innovation, new Scene, and genius born of a 'suffering' we somehow long to imagine, even as we co-opt, overpay, homogenize, make the best of that suffering song go to stud for our own pale performers.

So an easy analysis, through the fast train's glass, of rap as the latest occasion for the postliberal and highly vicarious guilt we find as exhilarating as it is necessary—that we like to play voyeur, play at being kept, for once, truly outside; it assuages, makes us think what's inside that torn-down world refers to us in no way, abides here decayed because Meant To, the pain of the snarling faces the raps exit no more relevant or real than the cathode guts of Our own biggest window. The white illusion of 'authenticity' as a signpost to equity, the sameness-in-indifference of '80s P.R.: Let Ghetto Be Ghetto, from the train.

Except but now here's what's neat: Step out, even just for a moment, and it turns out that this time it isn't the train that's moving, it's the gutted landscape of rap itself; and the 'ruins' that are its

---

[1] ...to say nothing of —courts!

home and *raison* aren't nearly the static archeology they seem, they themselves are moving, arranging themselves, becoming something no less bombed-out or dire but now somehow *intended from within*, a hegemony that matters, a self-conscious apposition, moving into expression, into Awareness, 'thriving' culturally somehow, copulating even; so that what had looked from the moving glass to be a place's and people's past-in-present reveals itself now a ruined totem to *total* presence — a separate, unequal, Other place-and-time, exploding outward.

Rap is the clattered kaboom of that explosion, itself expanding gaslike through '80s' dry time, growing from house-party schtick, gang anthem, a small-label fad with the sort of pop life span you measure with egg timers — then somehow, when We weren't looking, into scene, movement, On the Air — finally, in the last 24 months, assuming the fecund role of genuine Genre. Exploding into subspecies now faster than you can track. There's now Dub's mix of rap and reggae, House's mix of rap and '70s, huge-afro'd funk, Acid House's psychedelic hip-hop. There is black rap for white mass-consumption (Tone Lōc, Run-DMC), black rap for local set and house consumption (countless local stars and wannabes in every large city), ultrablack rap superstars for the whole marginal Nation inside (Heavy D, Public Enemy, Big Daddy Kane), white rap for white masses (the execrable Beastie Boys). There is Hispanic, Salsa-influenced rap out of different West Coast barrios, rap fused with West Indian or Islamic traditional music in Digital Underground, Eric B. & Rakim, and others, or fused with oh-so-danceable R&B in the 'new jack swing' offshoot (Bobby Brown, MC Hammer); even gay and bohemian young urban B-boys have their trendsetters in Teddy Riley and Guy, De La

Soul, Kwabe. Etc. etc.[2] A major impediment to sampling this Scene is the kaleidoscopic fury with which the Scene itself's changing. I.e., if you're reading this in print it's already dated.

And the rap world's vitality is one of replacement as well as variety, allowing the genre to remain fresh even as band after band is seduced into the 'real' music biz. This Scene's hydralike. The moment a rap artist like Run-DMC or L.L. Cool J 'breaks through' into major-market mix appeal, MTV's land of corporate bankability, certain reactions within the urban underground that spawned them can almost always be observed. The breakthrough band's B-boys themselves are without qualm about the pop big time: after all, they've been rapping all along about their entitlement to money and status, about the inevitable rewards of their freshness and unbiteable voice. Their postbreakthrough raps tend all too often to become celebrations of their new wealth and fame, of the now

---

[2]Note how the ecstatic force's movement extends beyond sound into dance— Chicago-based house dancing is very different from Coast-based rap dancing, while both are distinct from the Quaalude sway a De La Soul's lazy complexity invites— and beyond dance into urban haute couture itself. The 'cameo' or 'fade,' that troubling cyberpunk flat-top haircut favored by Carl Lewis and Grace Jones but popularized by the group Cameo's rapping Larry Blackmon, has now become less a haircut than a sculptural statement: words, logos, slogans, and complex signs razored into the rigid anvil of hair that is, according to the *Voice*, 'the most culturally conscious unisex hairstyle since the afro.' The standard '80s-rap uniform— sideways baseball cap or Kangol, ropy chains, acetate warm-up, and unlaced hightops—'now symbolizes a cruder, more casual era,' and is diffracting into a rap-House-gay-jackswing look replete with polka-dotties, loose pleated twills, and expensive dance loafers or British 'moon boots,' a combination Ricky Ricardo–Frank Sinatra dapper that now befits a Scene with the dignity, silliness, and pull of real Genre. Plus don't forget that just one big change in street and school fashions means millions and millions in garment revenue—even more $ once the white mainstream, as is its wont, follows in the cutting edge's media-delayed wake.

enhanced authority of their 'Message' — though it's hard to feature Public Enemy rapping about a Black Militant renaissance, about revolution and American apocalypse, while lily-white CBS Records pays them millions for the distribution rights to just such exhortations to cut corporate throats.

Nevertheless, back in the underground Scene, the breakthrough band's tight set of original fans tends to hang loyal, to await feverishly *'their'* crew's spots on the same music TV they love to dis. In short, there are (comparatively) few of the accusations of selling out that accompanied a similarly oxymoronic co-opting phenomenon in late-'60s protest rock. Which if you think about it is passing strange. The white mainstream Other against which serious rap aligns and defines itself makes the '60s 'Establishment' look downright benign. Apparently the devil's credit is solid, downtown. Maybe it's impossible to sell souls you don't believe anyone has anymore? Anyway, this is fortunately not the crux. Because all during this time of discovery and crossover and $ and self-celebration, whole *new* rap acts have just suddenly risen like exhalations from the streets to take the crossover artists' place as the new bona fide 'buzz,' the hotly fresh, in the original black house– and floating-club underground. This happens in Boston, NY, Philly, Chicago, Washington, L.A. The latest 'Hard' rap underground displacement might be of Ice T by N.W.A and of Public Enemy by Schoolly D, while the 'Soft' or song-of-myself rap battle is currently between platinum-selling L.L. Cool J, the 'Returning Ruler' Slick Rick, and pretty-boy newcomers Kwame and Bobcat. (The displacement of Tone Lōc by Young MC is not applicable here; rap designed for mass-white consumption has, by definition, no underground.)

Very often the fresh new usurper bands are several orders of magnitude harsher, harder, meaner than their precursors, their terminology and themes right over the edge into what even in '89 couldn't get airplay: N.W.A's real name, 'Niggaz with Attitude,' is one that no white DJ or requester can even mention without a cringe at how it'll sound; while their monster underground hit "Fuck tha Police," like Schoolly D's "Mr. Big Dick," seems almost designed to ensure radio/cable rejection and thus, at least for a while, a kind of intense racial locality, special appeal to a cognoscenti of B-boys and esoteric retailers, a def insulation against the white sirens of big labels. It's a refreshing (no pun) phenomenon to watch, but it's difficult and frightening to imagine how the (Crossover → Usurpation) trend can possibly continue much longer; viz.:

M.
(2D)

SOON RAP PUBLICISTS will face a problem their porn counterparts encountered over a decade ago. Every single shocking act of sex or pain
will have been 'done' symbolically, and, in the process, rap's audience will have acquired a taste for bloody novelty. The result: our
first 'snuff' rap record, which, rumor will have it, an actual person
died making. Editorial writers will be appalled, giving the new
snuff rappers the kind of jackpot of free publicity N.W.A enjoyed in
the spring of '89.

D.
(2E)

A LOT OF serious rap talks about the ends of things — illusions, lives, neighborhoods, rock 'n' roll, the World itself. If it is a true genre, it's one conspicuous for the darkness of its vision: a kind of dystopian present from which no imaginative future can even emerge. Long-honored musical 'messages' of hope, faith, reconciliation, of the importance of basic compassion, peace, spirituality, political (dare one say economic?) equality have, here as elsewhere in post-Reagan culture, been not just rejected but relegated to the status of an oh-come-on cliché, instant ridicule — cf. the implications of those damned involuntary quotation marks around 'messages.' A roll of jaded streetwise eyes at one's naïveté effectively disses even the politest requests to hear about rap music's 'vision of the future' or 'program for change'[1] — in the Scene such ideas are mutely regarded as either superannuated civil rights windmill-tilting or the glad-handing bullshit of the white politicians who, after all, built what rap lives in.

One of the serious rapper's standard stage personae, in fact, is that of speaker-of-the-Hard-sociopolitical-truth — 'The Warrior / Of Metaphor' as K-9 Posse puts it, or Chuck D's self-proclaimed rap title, 'Messenger of Prophecy' — the messenger who this time may not safely be blamed, for he brings with his news brass knuckles and gun. Many Hard-rap stars have ample preparation for this role of violent bellower, tough-as-nails prophet, the Angry Black Man. N.W.A's led by an admitted ex-gangbanger from the infamous make-sure-you-have-plenty-of-gas L.A. district of Compton. Schoolly D, too, is an alumnus of years in a Philly street gang. Former coke-racket enforcer Just-Ice, Washington's biggest rap name, came to New York and Art after being arrested by D.C. police on charges of murdering a rival dealer. Just-Ice has all gold teeth with his name spelled in gems across his incisors, and he was recently jailed again for sending a girlfriend to the hospital.

The angry political Malcolmite rapper is almost always the rapper-as-soldier, the -banger next door, his hard harsh shout a kind of relief from the dissing and self-satisfaction ('I'm ten times

---

[1]N.W.A has the latest last word here:

> *Do I look like a motherfuckin' role model?*
> *To a kid lookin up to me:*
> *I say life aint nothin but bitches and money.*

> —"Gangsta Gangsta" off *Straight Outta Compton*

deffer than the guy who claims he's ten times deffer than me') of Softer rap; but their self-consciously red edge leads Hard acts to some pretty strange defenses against the charge that they're justifying or even promoting urban violence. E.g., Public Enemy's Chuck D evinces complete seriousness in explaining that, in the opening lyrics to *Yo! Bum Rush the Show*'s third cut,

> *I show you my gun*
> *My Uzi weighs a ton*

the 'Uzi' actually means only the 'machine gun' of Public Enemy's *music,* of Chuck's own voice and message.

Now, if Chuck's cheek is tongueless, here, he's effected a weird (also brilliant, and scary) flip-flop of metonymy's enabling lyric-function in the traditional war of rock/rebellion vs. censor/order. It's well-known in pop history that slang and double entendre and even the tacit neologizing of innocuous words were used to make rock lyrics at once explicit or shocking enough to be 'rock' and suitable enough for the radio airplay rock needed — e.g.,

> *Baby, here is my love*
> *I'd just love to love you*

equals

> *Baby, here is my dick*
> *I'd just love to fuck you*

— so that the traditional rocker can grin and look innocently around and ask well gee what's so wrong with singing about *love?*

Chuck D's argument is a 180° on the pop-metonymy defense, here, and actually resembles closely a standard move in a different campaign, that of poststructuralist critics against the Thematic old guard in art and lit. Chuck D claims that 'Uzi' — which is surely the signifier of a real type of mow-down gun, one which for obvious reasons he probably shouldn't sing proudly about in '89 New York — is, in the lyrics, itself serving as nothing more than a *metonym for self-reference*. For Hard-rapper Chuck, something like

> *I rap you my stuff*
> *My lyrics take no guff*

...i.e., the song *itself* becomes the true deep referent in the meaning-layered lyrics of any music that wishes to enjoy the favors of outrage-hungry pop audience and conservative entertainment industry alike. This is a prototypical '80s-loop reversal, equivalent to arguing that singing 'Here is my dick' is innocuous because 'dick' is actually functioning as a metonym for the 'love' that informs what are 'really' just love-song lyrics. That the obversion seems absurdly circular is a fact about semantics and usage, not about the ambition and neat creativity of a rapper who would strip artistic terms of contexts so traditional they're pre-Greek.[2]

Most rapper personae, though, are pretty traditional themselves, or at least aren't trying to force anything like a revolution in the way performers' lyrics are heard and swallowed. Almost as common as the jeremiad-deliverer of Hard rap is another favorite persona: rapper-as-imp, as wily mariner, merry prankster, the

---

[2] Again: this is assuming Mr. D's serious; and it is sort of to Public Enemy's credit that it's often very hard to tell.

picaresque little hero who uses his wit and rap-creativity to best stronger or better-armed foes (here the enemies are always either other B-boys or police). The roots of this identity are traceable in just about any direction you like, from Jungian archetypology to *The Golden Bough* to Aesop; but the wily trickster's an especially beloved character in the folk tales of those West African nations whence the ancestors of many American blacks were invited to come explore New World career opportunities. I.e., Legba, the 'Blue Man' of the Yoruba tribe's didactic folk tradition, devil/sprite whose job is 'out-clevering' everyone he encounters, who is boastful, ruthless in victory, generous in rare defeat (and who is the namesake, some culturists argue, of nothing other than American 'Blues'), finds an almost direct late-'80s descendant in such memorable songs as our old friend Schoolly D's "Signifying Rapper," a new type of cut that opens up Hard rap's artistic possibilities even further, effecting an historical closure by which this high-tech genre insiders define as 'any rhythmic rhymes spoken over a strong beat' can perform its best-rooted and probably strongest function: storytelling.

"Signifying Rapper," recited to the digitally canonized krush groove of Led Zeppelin's classic "Kashmir" (itself a kind of allegoric ballad about 'Weird Journeys in an Alien Land'), is the story of an Everyrapper who, suffering repeated beatings at the hands of a certain 'bad-ass pimp' who kicks the little rapper 'all over the ghetto town,' decides finally to 'start using his wit' against his tormentor in hopes of ending 'this "kick-ass" shit.'[3] The rapper seeks

---

[3] ... a Reagan-era updating of an ancient West African tale about a trickster-monkey who baits a lion, which Schoolly D may have encountered in his dad's record collection on vocalist Oscar Brown Jr.'s early-'60s scat-classic "Signifying Monkey." — M.

the pimp out at dawn the next day and reports urgently that 'There's this mean, big *bad* faggot / Comin your way,' a faggot who's been putting down the pimp all over the projects. Under the narrative immunity enjoyed by any 'tale-teller'—someone who of course is just reporting the original words of another—the signifying rapper gets off an ad-libbed string of impeccably rhymed and stressed lines at the bad-ass pimp's expense, high-lights of which string include

> *He say he know your daddy, and he's a faggot*
> *And your mother's a whore.*
> *He say he seen you sellin asshole*
> *Door to door.*
> *Yeah, that's what he say.*
> *Listen to what else he say, Mr.* 'bad-ass pimp' —
> *He say: your granny? she's a dyke.*
> *And your other brother's a faggot.*
> *And your little sister Lu? She so low*
> *She suck the dick of a little maggot....*

...(that last line having become a special favorite in a certain Somerbridge apartment).

It's maybe natural in a rap we just plain like so much to see fruitful subtext all over the place—a covert legitimization of sampling, or of the artistic function of the Hard rapper himself—in "Signifying Rapper's" hook and moral: a person, even if small, marginal, and oppressed, can still say pretty much whatever he likes to whomever he wishes, and do it with impunity, so long as he has enough on the ball to present what's said as *message*, as intelligence from the field, a delivery from the heart and mouth of some Other (or maybe some group whom the oppressed imp is speaking *for*). The trick's all in whom the shit's presented as *for* and *from*, another matter of objects and preps.

At any rate, the device pays off handsomely for the S.R. himself. The pimp, enraged *by* the rapper's insults but of course *at* the putative source, arms himself and seeks out this huge, big-bad, heavy-leather 'faggot.' Except of course, once he finds the insults' 'source,' the pimp gets his gun taken from him in short order, has his bad ass handed to him

> *... in a hell of a way.*
> *Me myself, I don't know how he survived.*
> *Came back to the Projects more dead than alive.*

... Projects where the signifying rapper, who's now taken the pimp's whores and is standing triumphant and postcoital on top of 'one of them tall-ass Project buildings,' shakes his finger at his bad-ass tormentor and tells him, amid much electronic echo,

> *I shoulda kicked your ass*
> *My-motherfuckin-self.*

The "S.R." story itself is not exactly Dante, but the mix of cruel wit and silly pride is vintage Legba. And rapper-as-imp-hero conduces nicely to rap-as-*ballad,* the ancient mode that is quite likely rap music's destined best.

Closely related to both rapper personae above is that of impresario, smooth handler of crowds, the ad-libbing medium between music and ear, a carnival barker of defness and exhortation. Great examples are Russell Rush Simmons in "Cold Chillin' in the Spot," Eric B. in "Paid in Full's" last verse, and the Flavor Flav of "Rebel Without a Pause." It's probably safe to think of this as the rapper's original South Bronx identity, ad-lib bullshitting effortlessly over the stacked jams on the house or block party's tables. Rap's rhymed, precomposed lyrics, then, would be an innovation, the DJ's easement in his migration from host to costar, the prosody itself rooted in the urban black tradition of 'Ranking' or 'The Dozens,' in which two rivals exchange insults in straight rhyme and a driving ⅞ meter. (You can see early caucasian-translatable examples of The Dozens on old episodes of *The Jeffersons, Good Times,* and *Fat Albert and the Cosby Kids,* all ubiquitous on afternoon cable.)

Except for the hip-hop artists' fourth and dreariest guise, that of rapper-as-stud, much-beloved lover, enjoying epic-scale success with women either via outright misogyny, 'keeping da nasty bitches in line'—which, in the raps, the nasty bitches seem not only to stand for but believe it or not to *enjoy,* the single most nauseous feature of rap—or via portraying himself as just a big ole bloated love doll, lugubrious and eyelash-batting—see Tone Lōc's "Funky Cold Medina," Just-Ice's "Latoya," Bobby Brown's "My Prerogative," or the seminal self-parody of the Fat Boys in general—besides this all-too-common role, one that's too dull really to discuss, most of the other rapper identities are just subheadings, masks over masks. But the masks are many, too many for anything really but direct aural inspection: rap personae can change frequently even within single albums, the rapper delivering a Hard violent Black Nationalist communiqué on one cut, dubbing against Trinidadian steel drums on another, basking in big-label éclat on a third, cracking a head and then defly outwitting someone muscled and dumb, cooing to his 'bitch' and then on the flip side threatening to go get his gun again if she can't learn who's boss. Though any crew naturally wants its own distinctive game and face, the quintessential rap group is unquintessential, chameleonesque. This is either by weird design, or it's a symptom and symbol of chic contemporary facelessness... or most likely it's just a good old venerable synecdoche of rap's Genre itself, one that's now moving so fast it can't quite fix on its own identity... much less hold still for anything like cool critical classification or assessment, from outside.

3. ACQUISITION

Freedom is only true freedom when it appears against the background of an artificial limitation.

—*Eliot, "Reflections on Vers Libre," 1917*

A free African population is a curse to any country.... Negroes, in a state of freedom, and in the midst of a civilized community, become pilferers and marauders, consumers without being producers ... governed mainly by the instincts of animal nature.

—*Chancellor, South Carolina Courts of Appeals, in Cattarall (ed.)*
Judicial Cases, II, *1857*

...FREEDOM IS A ROAD SELDOM TRAVELED BY THE MULTITUDE FREEDOM IS A ROAD SELDOM TRAVELED BY THE MULTITUDE FREEDOM IS A ROAD SELDOM TRAVELED BY THE MULTITUDE FREEDOM IS A ROAD SELDOM TRAVELED BY THE MULTITUDE FREEDOM IS A ROAD SELDOM TRAVELED BY THE MULTITUDE

—*Public Enemy,* It Takes a Nation of Millions to Hold Us Back, *record jacket, all across lower border, 1988*

D.
(3A)

"IMPEDIMENT," then, turns out to be an apology for any outside sampler's inevitable simplification. By this summer, the generic rap that deserves to engage the Great Pop Masses — and at least the courtship's under way — has exploded so fast and hot it doesn't even exist anymore as any unitary rubric or genre...except as the sum of a very few features common to, and maybe comprehensive of, all the different rap subgenres and offshoots we've had to try to get some kind of rope around even to talk about. Crudely, what distinguishes rap *esse* for us is that it's a musical/antimusical form with:

 a) No melody besides canonized fragment w/o progression;

 b) A driving, oh-so-danceable $^4/_4$-cut-time 'krush groove,' a pyramidical rhythms-within-rhythms structure

DAVID FOSTER WALLACE and MARK COSTELLO

that's derivative both of the finger-in-the-air rhythm carpets of '70s disco and of funk's dance-renaissance rebellion against the antiphysical $^4/_4$ time of jazz—rap, like funk, appropriates jazz's bass melodies' hypnotic drive and $^4/_4$ adrenaline, but narrows the wide range of $^4/_4$ pulse patterns to the staccato'd $^4/_4$-cut that makes all great rock easy to move to;

c) Lyrics that are spoken or yelled, often rhymed or assonant, but always metered, complicating and complementing the marriage of back-bass, scratches, and drums, creating a dense diachronic *rhythmic* layering instead of the harmonic or contrapuntal synchronicities that have marked most Western music from Haydn to Heads;

d) A consistency in its deployment of maybe half a dozen themes, from: an updated Black Nationalism (Public Enemy, Schoolly D, B.D.P., Just-Ice); to a general hagiography of the rapper and his crew (L.L. and Kwabe and Slick Rick and at times just about everybody); to the political/artistic timidity of the black community in general and the executives of 'urban' labels and radio in particular (Ice T, 2 Live Crew, Kool Moe Dee, Public Enemy); to the unsuitability of women to be anything but receptacles for organs (N.W.A and L.L. and especially Slick "Treat Her Like a Prostitute" Rick); to a livid disdain for drug users and dealers (Schoolly D, N.W.A), one that's way more affecting than Just Say No bake sales from ladies in sable—or the antidrug anthoalbums pro-bono'd by pop elites and their consultants of image—because the rap perspective is of course street-level, nothing foreshortened by perspective or height, the disdain always real, hearably so: not a trace of *ex machina* in lyrics that decry chemicals not because they're evil, or socially outré, but because they stupefy and disspirit and emasculate before they kill;

  e) An overall aesthetic that mainstream pop critics and performers (notably Stanley Crouch and Mark Jenkins, and those repositories of asceticism and musical depth, Paul McCartney and Sting[1]) scorn as shallow and materialistic and self-referential. But one that (we opine) is probably the most revolutionary movement in ten dry and formulated years of rock, a movement not without similarities to postmodernism[2] in art, fiction, classical

---

[1] cf. MTV's "History of Rap" Special, 8 June 1989:

P. McC.: I get so bored with this so-called rap music. "I'm so rich, I have so much money." Me friends say *I* should make a rap record. I've more money than any of them. Most of us just don't feel a need to wear our income on our sleeve.

St.: ... to crow about it like they do. I've always enjoyed black music. ... This is the first black music I haven't liked. Not that I have anything *against* it. Don't get me wrong.

P. McC.: That's what they say. That if you don't like rap you don't like them. You don't like Negroes. You see what they're doing. They're using racism in a racist way themselves.

St.: They are not very original.

P. McC.: I could tape old Beatles material and move it around and play it back also, and sing about how much money it brings in.

St.: Anyone could. Is it music if anyone can do it?

[2] Does it get your goat when 'postmodernism' is tossed around as if everyone agreed on what it meant? Here is how we're deploying the term w/r/t serious rap, courtesy of *Dissent*'s Todd Gitlin:

Postmodernism is completely indifferent to questions of consistency and continuity. It self-consciously splices genres, attitudes, styles. It relishes the blurring or juxtaposition of forms, stances, moods, cultural levels. It

music, poetry. It's a new and carnivorous kind of mimesis that makes weary old 'self-reference' actually kind of interesting, because it enlarges Self from the standard rock-subjective—a bundle of hormone-drenched emotions attached to a larynx and pelvis—to a 'big ole head,' a kind of visual street-corner, a monadic Everybrother, an angry, jaded eye on a centerless pop-culture country full of marginalized subnations that are *themselves* postmodern, looped, self-referential, self-obsessed, voyeuristic, passive, slack-jawed, debased, and sources of such prodigious signal-and-data bombardment that they seem to move faster than the angry eye itself can see; an emptily expanding Bigness that can be described, much less transfigured, only by a mouth big and ill-mannered enough to try to take it all inside. Vitalists have argued for forty years that postwar art's ultimate expression will be a kind of enormous psychosocial excrement. The real aesthetic, conscious or otherwise, of today's best serious rap may be nothing but the first wave of this Great Peristalsis....

Anyway, all this stuff's a distinguishing feature, along of course with

f) No instruments. Nor even any original notes, really, at all, I'm afraid.

---

disdains 'originality' and fancies copies, repetition, the recombination of hand-me-down scraps. It pulls the rug out from under itself, displaying an acute self-consciousness about the work's constructed nature (Winter '89);

or, probably appropriater yet, of *Spy*'s Bruce Handy:

Basically, postmodernism is whatever you want it to be, if you want it badly enough (April '88).

Digital editing technology, the control over byte and combination it affords the user, is going to revolutionize home entertainment right around the millennium. You'll be able to watch a sampled *Lucy* show that's set in your own hometown, for example, or with yourself as Ricky, or hell even as Lucy *and* Ricky, if you want; or to mix and edit *Mr. Ed* into *Body Heat* and see a horse astride Kathleen Turner. The private home won't see serious digitals for at least a decade, though: the technology's too costly now for anyone but studio pros (while instruments, amps, TVs, even synthesizers are, like trendy aesthetic terms, available to pretty much whoever wants them badly enough).

As of now, digitals are at their most potent aurally: their use in record production is way more extensive than it is in video or film editing (even Lucas's/Spielberg's). But with the rare exceptions of such experimental, made-in-studio classics as Byrne and Eno's *My Life in the Bush of Ghosts*, rap/hip-hop has been the first important American pop to use digital recording and mixing techniques in the music's *composition*, its *soul*, instead of as just some heavy-art gesture.

To put it otherwise, serious '80s rap is the first 'music' composed entirely of notes created and performed, copyrighted and peddled, by precursors. The raw mainstream critical nerve here has to do with issues of originality vs. necessity. The fact that records and tapes were the only source of professional-quality sounds available to people unable to buy anything but prerecorded music and the equipment to listen...this is OK as an *historical* explanation of rap & sampling. Now, however, it's obvious that lots of rap groups, as evidenced by both their *Billboard* chart positions and their own exuberant lyrics, are able to afford not only the musical instruments they once couldn't get, but now the much *more* expensive digital equipment they'd before had to mimic homemade.

This quantum, middle-excluding leap from only-inexpensive-source-available to most-expensive-source-buyable, the complete bypass of the intermediate stage—viz., some kind of *original performance*—is surreally Algeresque: rags *or* riches—a vivid reflection, for the passing outsider, of a culture that seems now to have thoroughly dismissed the hidden middle-class assumptions behind a Great Society's upward-mobility-for-Negroes imperative.

Established evaluators of pop, though, still see the note-sampling situation only as what it is: some pretty strong elements of hypocrisy and laziness (we just *hate* them lazy) in wealthy black rappers who now use state-of-the-art technology they didn't invent to cut and paste music they didn't make—plus white-pop kelp they've absorbed as passively as We—into the kind of pretentious 'statement' '60s pseudo-artists who just pitched paint at the canvas sidearm used to refer to, vaguely, smugly. For mainstream critical purposes, these rappers are seeking to 'legitimate' themselves artistically via the history of rap's consignment to purchase, listening, and replay, a consignment to the very crude ghetto world the critic is quick to point out the rappers have now bought tickets out of, escaped, transcended via the 'art' that encourages precisely what's worst in the black urban world to thrive. Thus the rapper isn't artistically legit, doesn't 'create'; he merely regurgitates the popular art and artifacts his world has taken, or had imposed on it, as that part of the Self it can see. Many critics, especially in the Big Dis that is silence, direct at rappers the same distant pith that helped critics crush 'sample-heavy' literature—post-Beat and modern—back in the '70s, when rap was just a self-consumptive twinkle in funk's eye: cf. Morris Lurowitcz on John Barth's *Chimera:* 'unoriginality is as unoriginal…as exhaustion is tiring.'

Except there are more salient ways to criticize a self-consciously 'closed' music's obsessive use of samples that must by nature be open:

M.
(3B)

Free Sample 2

HARD RAP'S ANTHEMS of Black Supremacy are on often uncertain ground.
Public Enemy has seized every available source of militant non-
whiteness, without realizing that, in '80s-speak, when you sleep
with a source you sleep with everyone your source has slept with.
Chuck D doesn't see the danger he's in. He'd admit with pride a
debt to early rapper Afrika Bambaataa, a son of the Bronx who
founded an early-'60s afro-consciousness group called Zulu Nation.
But Bambaataa was, by his account, inspired by *Zulu,* a British-
made war movie starring Michael Caine. It's not that the Black
Panthers shot cops; it's that in spare moments between shootings
they dug folk music, drafting Power-to-the-People manifestos with
Bob Dylan's "Ballad of a Thin Man" revolving on the hi-fi. Dylan,
in fact, might be Public Enemy's unacknowledged papa, for he was

rapping back when LBJ was the Antichrist and Ed Koch was a hungry young reformer.

Public Enemy's calculatedly outrageous talk (cf. Professor Griff's infamous 'Why do you think it's called *jewelry?*' *Washington Times* interview) owes a debt to the self-promoting '60s, when the Black Panthers posed for *Time* magazine toting borrowed, unloaded shotguns. Before the Panthers there was Dylan, showing up for a major press conference in Mad Hatter costume, carrying a jumbo lightbulb, telling an audience soon after JFK's death that he saw some of himself in Lee Oswald. There's John Lennon, in the hysteria surrounding the Beatles' 1964 arrival in New York City, saying that the Fab Four were bigger than Jesus Christ, later lamely backpedaling, claiming that he'd really just meant that the Beatles sold more *records* than Jesus Christ. So too P.E. backpedaled from Professor Griff's antisemitism, first telling interviews he didn't mean it, then that he didn't speak for the group, then firing Griff from the band and refusing comment altogether, later backpedaling from their backpedaling, quietly reinstating Griff in a limited role.

Fifteen years after Bob Dylan stopped wearing his Mad Hatter top hat, Public Enemy's Flavor Flav showed up on the set of the "Fight the Power" video wearing sweats, shades, and—yes—his very own Mad Hatter top hat. Fifteen years before MCs adopted outrageous monikers like Just-Ice, Ice T, Ice Cube, Mix Master Ice, Robert Zimmerman dubbed himself Bob Dylan, sampling the name from twin loves, the poet Dylan Thomas and the TV lawman Matt Dillon. Later, having remastered an American self, Robert Zimmerman became a counterculture star singing poetry and dressing like a cowboy.

Long before digital multitracked sampling erased boundaries between genres, we were all multitracking in our heads, sampling together everything we ever saw on TV or heard in stereo, including stuff made by people who, before making it, loved the TV and music we ourselves had loved, and couldn't help but sample it, just as Aerosmith so loved the Stones they couldn't help but copy them. Long before rap began to pillage shared culture, we did it: walking like James Dean while talking like Jack Nicholson, looking for a woman who could show cleavage the same sly way Marilyn did. Traffic in influence booms. Disciples multiply like AIDS cases, like hiss begetting hiss on early studio remixes. In explosively mass-sold music, implications and applications are uncontrollably everywhere: there is first 1 band called the Rolling Stones, then 2 Rolling Stones copycat bands, begetting 4 who copy the copiers, begetting 8, 16, 32, 64. This math unfolds nightly on MTV: keeping score is the last fascination remaining there.[1]

Stranded after 30 years of pop music's wildcatting and copycatting, P.E. cannot locate even one pure black source. It's no wonder that rap seeks freedom in mangling its yesterday. It's no wonder that rappers hooked on violent rhymes also make the wildest, most riotlike use of sampling technology. And, given the oppression-by-influence that all races raised with TV feel, it's no wonder

---

[1]Somewhere in the Midwest, kids sit watching music videos & playing a drinking game called 'MTV,' which is swiftly supplanting Russian roulette and chicken fights as *the* teenage danger game. The game's rules:

(1) IF a lame white boy (badly) rips off Muddy Waters's famous solo from "Mannish Boy," YOU chug half a Bud; UNLESS the lame white boy is too dumb to know who Muddy Waters is (or was), in which case YOU chug the whole Bud;

(2) IF on the other hand, the lame white boy (badly) rips off Mick Jagger ripping off Muddy Waters, YOU chug the whole Bud; UNLESS the lame white boy *is* Mick Jagger (badly) ripping off Mick Jagger, in which case it's a Bud commercial, in which case YOUR punishment: watch.

that these same rappers enjoy the largest, unhappiest white audience.

Mark, then, this sitcom as rap turns ten, this Shakespearean garden farce of disguise and recognition, ending when you see that your enemy is your ally, or yourself—that you never really even *had* enemies.

Where will this recognition of rap's deep whiteness leave Public Enemy? They'll be Public Friend, rapping "The Star-Spangled Banner" before the opening game of the '99 World Series. And it goes a little something like this.

M.
(3C)

Whose Pavlovs Are These?

RAP'S SONIC VIOLENCE is child of the clash of styles and nodes of the associations audiences attach to these styles,[1] with Sunbeam-Mixmaster MC as malevolent, accident-orchestrating traffic cop.

Sampling is, after all, the unauthorized re-use of a sound you

---

[1]These 'nodes of associations' we call 'pavlovs'—a unit of measure of everything we feel or think while hearing music we've heard before.

Pavlovs can be formed in as many different ways as we can come to love anything. Fucking to an album makes you love that album forevermore (unless of course the woman you were with later breaks your heart into many small pieces, in which case you'll come to pavlov—yes, it's also a verb—the album with pain and hate it for all time). Aesthetically, pavloving shouldn't happen, but in experience it does. Thus at least two young Bostonians alive as of this writing cannot listen to, say, Side A of the 10,000 Maniacs' *In My Tribe* in any context without feeling things more pungent than anything sanely attributable to the Maniacs.

don't own. It's outlaw commerce, related by marriage to the billion-dollar service sector in drugs currently flourishing in the very Urban Enterprise Zones where ten years of Republicanism have failed to seed legal business. The many-part mix, more freeing and unsettling than any one element if heard alone, is more potent when adulterated, like crack'd cocaine: a spark of riots.

There is, of course, a genre at least as elaborate and closed as the sitcom, one called Intellectual Property, a branch of law purporting to regulate traffic in all other genres, which maintains that those who make genres—who write scripts, cut songs, compose pseudo-Bedouin schlock—have proprietary rights to these scripts, songs, and schlock. But rap sparks riots here, too, leaving shakier the very basis of organized music: control of final product.

Suits pending in New York courts involve white rappers the Beastie Boys' sampling of the two words 'Yo' and 'Leroy,' along with a bit of backbeat, from Jimmy Castor's 1977 hit "The Return of Leroy (Part I)." It is undisputed that the Beastie Boys taped a tape of Castor's voice saying the words 'Yo Leroy' as part of the sound carpet in the cut "Hold It Now, Hit It" from their smash *Licensed to Ill* LP. The Beasties' defense of an otherwise blatant infringement on Castor's ownership of the sound, taped or otherwise, of his own voice is that Castor had himself ripped off a series of popular 'Leroy' songs that he did not own. 'It appears the only new element in the song the Beastie Boys sampled is the word "Yo,"' an attorney for the Beasties told the *National Law Journal* in February '89. 'The question then becomes, can you have a proprietary right to the word "Yo"?'

Pavlovs are everything we come to associate with music—and can reexperience in listening again—that isn't 'in' the music. They're what we each bring to bear, when rightly cued. Pavlovs are the saliva that flows when the bells ring.

Can you own 'Yo'? Infringement of a protected work—like Jimmy Castor's "Return of Leroy" or Tam-Tam's "I'm Cryin"—generally requires a showing that the purloined snippet of the pre-existing piece constitutes the 'essence' of that piece. If a funky bass-line is the essence of funkist Castor, then even a handful of notes put to dramatically new-sounding use is an infringement that Castor could get a court order to halt. It's the legal difference between quotation (which is OK) and plagiarism (which isn't). It's also one of those lovely metaphysical notions—that art has an 'essence' that can and must be 'protected'—that wandered into intellectual property law and was trapped there.

No judge has yet written a decision defining the copyrightable essence of funk, and they don't seem to be lining up to do so. A pity. We await the day when rap's infringements supplant *Roe v. Wade* as hot jurisprudential potato, when federal judicial appointees face rough Senate confirmation hearings because of previously published opinions that James Brown's between-verse habit of saying *'Huh' wasn't* 'essential' to the heavy funk.[2]

Rules about the ownership of an artistic work, which apply

---

[2] . . . when a big-jowled Dixiecrat Senator leans into the microphones to ask, mock-incredulous: 'Now, Mr. Costello, isn't it in fact the case that you once cowrote and also authored a book published under the title *Significant Wrapper,* in which you argued that Mr. Brown's habit of saying "Huh" and "Smokin'" and "Give it here" and "GoodGod" (pronounced as if it were one word) was *not,* in your opinion, ee-sen-shul to the cold dead heavy funk as practiced and popularized by my fellow native son of Georgia, Mr. Brown? In fact,' the Dixiecrat waxes prosecutorially, 'isn't it true that you stated in the pages of this alleged book that you considered the guitar work of Bobby Byrd, *and not the individual named James Brown at all,* to be the essence of that music we call "James Brown"?'

At which point Mr. Costello, eyes on the prize of a cushy lifetime judicial appointment, squirms and offers smally: 'Yes.'

adequately to such static objects as this book, apply not at all to music. By making radically new use of old sounds, rap confounds intellectual property law as it confounds critics, sitcoms, heavy metal, Black Power, and whatever else it tosses in its blender, exposing a set of truths the music industry has kept nicely under wraps: you can't sell what you don't own; you don't own what you can't control; and, in an era of mass-consumed digital mixing and playback, you can't control the re-use of recorded sound.

Consider, for example, the leading case for our purposes, *Midler v. Ford Motor Company*, in which a federal court ruled that pop star Bette Midler could halt unauthorized use of her own 1972 version of "Do You Want to Dance?" and also versions of the same song sung by a similar-sounding woman.

Young & Rubicam Advertising had sold Ford on a far-fetched scheme called 'The Yuppie Campaign,' a series of 19 TV spots in which sleek new Fords prowl the roadways as a soundtrack of '60s soft-rock classics reminds us mistily of being 16. The campaign was genius, since we pavlov Fords with dads and rock with kids. The ad, linking Fords to rock, relaxed momentarily the horrible, if false, yuppie tensions: conformity vs. rebellion; maturity vs. youth; signing on vs. dropping out.

Midler refused to rerecord the song or to allow use of her 1972 version. Undeterred, Ford bought the rights to the song—though not to Midler's version of the song—and hired the immortal Ula Hedwig, who sounded eerily like Midler, to record it.

Midler v. Ford Motor Company ruled that Ford could not cash in

---

Now the Dixiecrat Senator bears down: 'And what's all this I hear about you leaving phone messages on the machine of a Jamaican drug kingpin's front company back in 1989?'

on all that Bette had worked so hard to come to mean to America, even if through a soundalike. *Midler* might make sense as a model of musical ownership, unless one thinks for even a nanosecond about the procedures of pop music. True, Midler touched many future yuppies with her 1972 "Do You Want to Dance?" But Bobby Freeman first recorded "Do You Want to Dance" in 1958, topping the charts for the tiny Jubilee label. Wasn't Midler herself pirating the party-time pavlovs Americans in '72 associated with the Eisenhower-era hit they remembered from 15 years before? Take it a step further. Bobby Freeman ripped off the Latin chord sequence that was the guts of his "Do You Want to Dance" from traditional Mexican musicians playing in the L.A. barrios.

A song that reminded Ford-buying yuppies in 1984 of going barefoot and smoking joints reminded a war-weary nation in 1972 of twistin' at sock hops, and sounded to those at the sock hops in 1958 like a seductive invitation to south-of-the-border sun and fun. If Ford owes monetary damages to Bette Midler for mining America's feelings about her "Do You Want to Dance?" then Bette Midler owes damages to Bobby Freeman for his "Do You Want to Dance" and Bobby Freeman owes damages to the entire legacy of *baion* music whence he took his famous chord sequence, and thus to each musician whose individual work kept that tradition alive long enough for Bobby Freeman to rip it off.[3] Closing the weird circle is

---

[3] A PLEA FROM D.

Bette Midler's intuition — which I share — is that there's some fundamental difference between: (1) pirating a piece of music and its attendant pavlovs for *artistic* reasons; and (2) doing so, as Ford seems to, as part of a cold, calculated effort to increase sales of a *product*. Well, but except the 'art' of popular music appears quite often as records, tapes, and CDs, which of course are themselves saleable. Does that mean that songs, like Fords, are all and only products? Which is the product, in

the fact that Ritchie Valens, born Richard Valenzuela, learned the Latin chord sequences that were a part of his Mexican heritage, and on which Valens based his '59 crossover hit "La Bamba," from Freeman, a black man.

To whom should pop — this widely shared, widely borrowed music — belong? Whose pavlovs are these?

pop — the sounds or the containers they come in? Does it make a difference? If you, like me, are insistent about an important distinction between Ford's use of Midler's pavlovs and Midler's use of (or tribute to, or comment on, or response to) Freeman's pavlovs, can you articulate what that distinction is in some way that isn't circular, or hideously digressive from this whole sampler's subject, or so freaking long it can't even be a way-too-long footnote? Any reader who can do so will be invited over to Somerbridge for a rousing game of MTV with D. and M. Simply send your articulated distinctions, in let's say 20 pages or fewer, to:

DISTINCTION BETWEEN ARTISTS RIPPING OFF
OTHER ARTISTS AND ADS DOING SO
D. Wallace & M. Costello
c/o
Ocean Records
134 Warren Street
Roxbury, MA 02154

D.
(3D)

WELL BUT TAKE heart. What are *indisputably* original, besides the particular (re-)arrangement of recorded sounds a rap band's digital hands help shape and create, are of course the cut's lyrics, the rap's *rap*, delivered by the MC/DJ in either straight rhyme, near-assonance, or the occasional ad-lib of stressed logorrhea. The rap's lyrics are bound to the sample-heavy 'song' behind by the quality and often ingenious complexity of their rhythmic relation. In a pretty obvious way, one that no reviewer seems ever to note, the metric, rhythmic possibilities the rapper's monologue explores are often what makes a particular cut driving and creative, in spite of—and see *because of*—the severe limitations of theme and near-cognate rhyme the genre imposes.

Understood as constraints, rap's rhyme-requirements are fertile w/r/t humor, and can often force the extra linguistic creativity that makes a good rap a great rap, one that won't leave your head.

For example, despite its shameless repetitive loop of Led Zep's most famous progression, the 24-note lead line of "Kashmir," Schoolly D's "Signifying Rapper" is a truly great song, partly because Mr. D's rhythmic and syntactic dash-and-stretches for acceptable rhymes within the narrative constraints of real story—the improbable vocab, vocal enjambments, counterstresses, metrical variations—counterpoint wonderfully the lyric's story's own delineation of rapper-as-ghetto-imp, nimbly at home in threatening surroundings he didn't create, able to thrive via 'wit' like a rabbit in brambles.

This all means that the rapper's lyric, to succeed, must function simultaneously: as the quickest, interval-inhabiting part, the human part, of the many-geared rhythmic machine that comprises most serious raps; as a powerful, shocking, repulsive, or witty monologue, as defness-in-motion; and as a formally clean and to-the-rhyme's-bone-hewing arrangement of a verse that, were it ever to come under review by today's senescent guardians of prosodic standard, would surely be dissed by them as either children's poetry or the sort of antediluvian form[1] that's interesting only as a limit 'modern' poetry has so completely transcended that adherence has ceased to be any criterion but dire, anti- (i.e., though rhyme's absence today doesn't guarantee 'good serious poetry,' its irony-free presence, today, ensures Hallmark-caliber doggerel).

Any kind of close listening, though, reveals that the best raps are usually operating in a high gear of poetical efficiency *against* the almost Eliotically strenuous limitations of both complex rhythmic demand and the requirement of near-cognate rhyme; the limitations here are the invaluable constraints of form that all good new art helps define itself by struggling against from inside them—the

---

[1] a form I've heard called variously 'straight' rhyme, 'rigid' rhyme, and 'AA' rhyme.

formal Other all 'fresh' speech needs. Straight rhyme, for example, is such a stiff formal cincture that in rap it necessitates really complicated prosodic innovations—disordered but effective enjambment, stresses alternated between standard feet, wild combinations of iamb with trochee and of both with spondee, the kind of metrical libertinism that spells f-r-e-e v-e-r-s-e but is here required by *exactly* the sort of tight aural walls free verse was all about knocking down.

Plus it's not hard to see that the coldly manufactured, self-consciously derivative sound carpet of samples over which the rapper and DJ declaim serves to focus listeners' creative attention on the complex and human lyrics themselves. The pop tradition by which rhythm and lyric became melody's supporting cast is here inverted. The rap is primarily *the rap:* that which is *said* must in hip-hop be the intraScenic locus of assessment, appreciation, complaint. So a thesis: the theme, energy, wit, and formal ingenuity of the rap[2] are where any meanly dressed, unMarginal spectator outside the window will and must look for aesthetic access to a music self-defined as not for him. That is, the outside listener must not only take the rap 'on authority'; he must *read* that rap as *story.*[3]

---

[2] ...together with this intangible quality about certain rappers—Rakim, Big Daddy Kane, Chuck D, Schoolly—whose personality sort of *forces* the rap on the listener's own personality...what is this thing? 'stage presence'? studio presence? genuine defness?...ne sais quoi?

[3] Raps that make this demand especially explicit include Schoolly's beloved "Signifying Rapper," Slick Rick's new "Bedtime Story," Public Enemy's "Sophisticated Bitch," and Boogie Down Productions' "Why Is That?"—this last cut an eerie Old Testament exegesis that goes about making white South Africans' favorite argument for them—blacks are the descendants of Cain—but adds a couple of ominous caveats: first, that they're descendants of *Cain,* not *'caine;* second, that Cain was just one *bad* mothafucka, one with a short fuse and no compunction about offing folks (like South Africans) who dissed him or pissed him off....

D.
(3E)

EVERY SERIOUS RAP has a theme.

Or, if your alternative to personal yuppiness is being avant-garde, the serious rap places the very theme of 'theme' under erasure — ~~'theme'~~ — by being, in fact, not just smug, whiny, or belligerent, but actually self-conscious and radical enough overtly to address the very contexts of history and marginalization that have already 'read'[1] the black and white communities in the racial/political/sexual/economic prejudices we respectively bring to rap's hearing. Rap, under close scrutiny, becomes 'critic-heavy' — a unique pop opportunity for the application of Marxist & poststructural principles to the cultural *production,* not just *reception,* of texts, lyrics, art (cf. Schoolly D's vinyl quotation of Gil Scott-Heron's

---

[1] Derrida's infamous *lissance*

record "The Revolution Will Not Be Televised," N.W.A's "Fuck tha Police," Ice T's "Rhyme Pays"). Rap is the self-conscious–self-consciousness loop academic feminists and deconstructionists drool over—and often the loop's *right there on the music's surface,* less to be rooted out truffle-like by the eager interpreter than the result of much such rooting by the rapper himself. But so rap, in its love of the *overtly* complex, often usurps the ('serious') outside critic's hallowed interpretive function: little wonder few licensed determiners of seriousness seem much disposed to take rap seriously. Just don't be duped by their rationale. Especially today, the unsubtle does not necessarily mean the simple or crude.

It'd be silly to claim that any of the street artists at issue here give one hoot about these abstractions and -isms; but this (again) doesn't mean rap-as-genre doesn't afford, through its unsubtle systems of self- and cultural reference, valuable fodder for the 'intellectual' willing to listen; nor that rap as art doesn't maybe deserve heavyweight critical attention, since so much of serious rap, like serious criticism itself, is all about creativity-within-contexts. The rapper is constantly boasting about what he can achieve with just

> *A pen and a paper,*
> *A stereo or tape or...*[2]

His chief criteria for dissing other hip-hop artists are not only those artists' 'illness' of composition but their *raps* themselves—'rap' here meaning the scansion and recital of what's composed, the defness needed to force black-audience acceptance of the MC's dual roles *of*

---

[2]Eric B. & Rakim, "Paid in Full (Seven Minutes of Madness)"—extended-play mix off the *Colors* soundtrack LP, 1988.

and *for,* the *je ne sais* required to lead-as-part-of;...in other words, and these are straight out of what defines good poets since like around Homer, to be a real rap artist is to have a Voice; for nothing does the genre have more scorn than for the 'tired' or 'lame,' the quiescent or mute.

Our opinion, then, from a distance: not only is a serious rap serious poetry, but, in terms of the size of its audience, its potency in the Great U.S. Market, its power to spur and to authorize the artistic endeavor of a discouraged and malschooled young urban culture we've been encouraged sadly to write off,[3] it's quite possibly the most important stuff happening in American poetry today. 'Real' (viz. academic) U.S. poetry, a world no less insular than rap, no less strange or stringent about vocab, manner, and the contexts it works off, has today become so inbred and (against its professed wishes) inaccessible that it just doesn't get to share its creative products with more than a couple thousand fanatical, sandal-shod readers, doesn't get to move or inform more than a fraction of that reader-ship (most of the moved being poets themselves), doesn't generate revenue for much of anyone save the universities to whom the best Ph.D. poets rent their names and time...and *especially* does not inspire a whole culture's youth to try to follow in its Connecticut-catalogue brogan's prints. Because of rap's meteoric rise, though, you've got poor kids, tough kids, 'underachievers,' a 'lost genera-tion'...more young people—ostensibly forever turned off 'lan-guage' by TV, video games, and low U.S.D.E. budgets—more of these kids hunched over notebooks on their own time, trying to put

---

[3]'We've lost a whole generation [to their own culture] out here,' rues an LAPD Assis-tant Commissioner in a 14 May '89 Boston TV news special on the national War On gangs, drugs, crime, Others....

words together in striking and creative ways, than the U.S.A. has probably ever had at one time. That few of these will become 'stars' matters far less than the grim stats about, say, the tiny percentage of playground basketball phenoms who actually ride sports out and up from subclass status: the same verbal skills and enthusiasms rap values (and values enough to let rap-dissing stand symbolically for fighting or killing) can obviously be applied in mainstream-approved, 'productive' ways — G.E.D.s, college, Standard Written English...perhaps someday even ad copywriting!

But so is this wildfire of urban rap-ambition raging around converted four-car garages like North Dorchester's RJam's *in spite* of the genre's near-disciplinary prosodic restrictions, or — as an Eliot would have it — *because* of them? Can't really tell. Probably doesn't matter. The fact remains that, were 'important poetry' presently defined in terms of what makes important art important in a Supply Side democracy (popularity, effect, the separation of fan from his cash), staid journals like *Poetry* and *American Poetry Review* would be featuring some number of fade-cut, multiple-earring'd authors' photos in each issue; and highbrow public readings would always carry their back-row faction of -bangers ready to 'listen rude' to Wilbur and Levertov and Ashbery, just as, e.g., Rimbaud and Pound did to their own contemporaries...to the delight and invigoration of a time's poetry....

...And even just the prospected fantasy of seeing Public Enemy's be-clocked Flavor Flav and like a Robert Bly or Amy Clampitt sitting down over beer and Celestial Seasonings to hash out the debate over line breaks in dactylic hexameter, a very serious young homeboy in Italian silk and pentagonal shades serving as interpreter, is enough to make us hereby officially lobby for the admission of rhyme's renaissance — at least under the stringent rhythmic demands rap has forced on rhyme-as-form—to the cold corridors of Serious Appreciation.

Unlike the mostly docile poetry and fiction of the late '80s, though, rap's own quality, the def freshness of the MC's bit, is set up to be judged primarily in the context of what it is *against*. In case you thought we forgot, rap is first of all a movement in rock music, and thus the time-honored requirement is that the rap Scene set itself very consciously athwart those circumstances and forces whose enormity is required by all rock 'n' roll to justify one of its essential roles, rebellion-against. Except now watch the objects of the rebellion alter, spread, grow in urgency—from the '50s' parents and principals, homework, hot rods, the sweet hurt of teen love, to the urban '80s' police, violent death, homelessness, the lure of ecstatic drugs that dehumanize, weaponry, fatherlessness, the animal emptiness of sex w/o love, the almost Trilaterally sinister white Establishment ('THE GOVERNMENT'S RESPONSIBLE THE GOVERNMENT'S...'), *Everyone Else:* life as a series of interruptions from an angry slumber about what the electric voices say you must have and what the human voices say you may not, about the betrayal of the past, of the promises exacted by Carmichael, X, and the now formal martyrdom of King. As in

M.
(3F)

The Freedom Rappers

THE HARDEST MCS—Schoolly D, Public Enemy's Chuck D, Eazy-E and MC Ren of N.W.A—share a family secret: they need the cops badly. Public Enemy's "Bring the Noise" fantasizes about being busted by TV policeman Steve McGarrett; elsewhere, Chuck's warned of an FBI wiretap on his telephone. N.W.A was lionized on Page 1 of the *Village Voice* as the target of a "Culture Crackdown" after an FBI peon sent a letter to N.W.A's label expressing concern over N.W.A's hit "Fuck tha Police," even though the *Voice* seemed to agree with the FBI on the merits of the music.

There's unexpected precedent for pros- and persecution as credential. In July 1962, Martin Luther King was convicted in a Georgia court of parading without a permit during nonviolent demonstrations against segregated public transportation in Albany, Georgia. Given a choice between a $178 fine and 45 days in jail,

King chose jail. He had served only one day when he was told that an anonymous 'well-dressed Negro' had paid the $178 fine. King protested; he wanted to stay jailed. The Albany police chief refused, explaining that since King's fine had now been paid, it would be illegal to keep him behind bars. The 'well-dressed Negro' was a fiction invented by segregationist police as an excuse to release King, whose stature grew with each day jailed. The well-dressed-Negro ploy would be one of the few strategies effective against nonviolent protest, getting civil rights leaders off the streets overnight without allowing them the symbolic martyrdom of a well-publicized prison term.

Chuck D's frequent brushes with the law are, of course, parables starring himself, designed to dramatize the evils of The System. But King did actual time as a symbol for the actual injustice of segregation. For Public Enemy, everything's symbol.

Public Enemy runs a kind of race-to-be-baddest begun by L.L. Cool J, the biggest rapper of '87, whose "I'm Bad" describes an NYPD manhunt with L.L. as subject. The baddest being the blackest being somehow the most 'real.' Badness being measured not by the Top 40, but rather by the 10 Most Wanted. Except that Public Enemy, no outlaws, work for Def Jam Records, which works, yes, for CBS, and so actual, profitable rap records tell of symbolic cop trouble.

But both P.E. and L.L. will inevitably lose the Badness Race as other, hungrier posses up the ante. The jacket photo of *Straight Outta Compton*, a notorious bit of pretend-gangbanging by L.A.'s N.W.A, shows the group's members standing over the face of whoever holds the album (camera positioned at the rappers' feet). A revolver is pointed at the album-holder's face, a photographic death threat against N.W.A's potential audience. Q.B.C., a Brooklyn-based rap act, isn't as subtle. Their "Back to School," a 12-inch released in '88 on Capitol's Mantronik label, features the trio on the jacket holding their teacher, a withered, middle-aged white woman, hostage at Uzipoint. Which says nothing more than this: rappers read the tabloids and the ads in the tabloids. American Express moves plastic with the fearful tagline *Don't leave home without it,* and Oxy-5 sells its gold-plated acne cure by asking *What do you want, a few more pennies or a few more zits?* as if Oxy-5 could visit zits on the doubting. Rappers have merely wised up to the fact that crisis is the best salesman.

In this, rappers sample a strategy from the civil rights movement. 'We planned the Freedom Ride with the specific intention of creating a crisis,' a key civil rights leader later said. The point was to do innocent things—travel, wait, eat—that somehow spurred beatings and bombings not otherwise a part of normalcy under segregation, but implicit in the ugliness of the system. 'To cure injustices,' King said, 'you must expose them before the light of human conscience....' You must, in short, dramatize brutality by provoking it. Drama is power.[1] The Freedom Riders succeeded in creating a crisis: activists were arrested for waiting in the white half of Greyhound terminals across Dixie. On May 14, 1961, Freedom Riders were attacked by a white mob outside Anniston, Alabama. The windows of their bus were smashed, and a firebomb was lobbed inside. A photograph of the burned bus, among the most famous images to come out of the civil rights struggle, was Page 1 news across the North, beginning the

---

[1] At least five feature-length films have depicted nonviolent protest in action, translating drama-as-power into powerful drama. These include the made-for-TV offering *Attack an Terror: The FBI vs. the Ku Klux Klan* starring Wayne Rogers; *The Autobiography of Miss Jane Pittman* with Cicely Tyson; 1983's cinematic release *Gandhi; King,* a made-for-TV effort starring Paul Winfield; and 1988's *Mississippi Burning.*

The drafting and enactment of the Civil Rights Act of 1964, an event of equal or greater significance in the struggle against discrimination, has never been the subject of a dramatic presentation.

swing in public opinion that would lead to the passage of major equal-protection legislation in the mid-'60s.

Rappers recycle the crisis-as-drama insight of the civil rights movement, but in re-using the insight they alter it crucially. Civil disobeyers commit crimes fraught with drama; rappers commit drama fraught with crime.

It should not surprise, given rap's almost poignant need for police harassment, that sampling, the mother methodology, is itself understood in-Scene as an outlaw credential. In "Caught, Can We Get a Witness?" Chuck D imagines a copyright-infringement lawsuit that's just another system crisis in a series of 'crimes' that, played like a movie, would open with Rosa Parks refusing to sit in the back of a Montgomery bus in '55, pan back to take in the triumphant Montgomery bus boycott that her refusal triggered, cut to the Freedom Rides in '61, the March on Washington in '63, the murder of King in '68, Tawana Brawley, Howard Beach, the Bensonhurst beatings of '89, and now Chuck D's own court date, a hassle that becomes, in rap logic, Law's attempt to silence a dangerous critic:

> *Caught, now in court 'cause I stole a beat*
> *This is a sampling sport*
> *But I'm giving it a new name*
> *What you hear is* mine
> *P.E., you know the time*
> *Now, what in the Heaven does a jury know about Hell*
> *If I took it, but they just look at me*
> *Like, Hey I'm on a mission*
> *I'm talkin' 'bout conditions*
> *Aint right sittin' like dynamite*
> *Gonna blow you up and it just might*

Blow up the bench and
Judge, the courtroom plus I gotta mention
This court is dismissed when I grab the mike. . . .

But what will Chuck D do when the plaintiff in the lawsuit to silence rap is not the KKK or the FBI or even the NYPD, but rather black musicians of his father's generation whose lifework he and his peers re-use? What will Chuck D do when he realizes that his enemy is his friend?

When rap tangles with the fathers of funk for the right to party, it won't be the first family split over the division of heirlooms. Carter-era economists clucked about the social impact of a shrinking economic pie. Ominous tracts detailed what would happen when Americans began to realize that there would, year after year, be fewer jobs at lower pay. A clash of the races and rising antisemitism were foretold. When the Great Recession ended in '83, the shrinking-pie analogy was given a merciful rest. The family fight over the rights to soul and funk, which has Chuck in "Caught" calling his rivals *Tom,* is just a single episode of an unfolding drama reminiscent of the '70s disappearing economic dessert: an '80s shrinking *cultural* pie where ever more would-be communicators fight to re-use ever fewer unspent symbols. Tommy Boy released "No Sell Out," Malcolm X orating over a sparse beat programmed by Keith LeBlanc, a percussionist involved with rap since before '79's "Rapper's Delight." Sugarhill, LeBlanc's old employer, sued Tommy Boy for infringement of Sugarhill's alleged rights to Malcolm X, and others grumbled about the sale of a black radical by a white drummer and his white-owned label. Rap like "No Sell Out" may be the best place to watch the Big Shrink breed rivals and ugly epithets, but examples abound in ads, politics, rock, movies, publishing. Megastar Madonna's whole gift

consists of evoking not one, but several Femmes We Remember
(Marilyn Monroe M, Tu, and Th; Jean Seberg W and F; Gidget on
the weekends). A survey found that 70% of the radio on FM—*FM*
mind you, Young America's megahertz—was some form of 'Oldies'
or 'Classic Rock' programming. Vietnam movies get made at the
rate of about three a year.

There were weeks in Iowa in 1988 when Joe Biden, Richard
Gephardt, and Michael Dukakis vied to varyingly rephrase a single
sentence spoken by John Kennedy on Inauguration Day, 1961: *Ask
not...* Even Republicans like Jack Kemp, sworn to dismantle the cogs
and belts Kennedy erected, strive for Kennedy-esqueness, attempting to use Kennedy as adjective to undo Kennedy as noun. Jesse
Jackson sounds different, and sells himself to white America as an
Alternative. But just as Topeka had dual, separate, 'equal' schools,
one white, one not, so too the reformist tumult of the '60s had dual,
separate, equal John Kennedys, one of whom was named Martin
Luther King. Or if you prefer: dual Kings, one named Kennedy.
Jesse Jackson sounds like an alternative to Gepbidekakis largely
because he siphons off the black half of the same scarce source. *I have
a dream,* Jackson the Alternative was telling surprised Iowans.

There was blood on Jesse Jackson's shirt the morning after Martin Luther King was shot on the balcony of the Lorraine Motel in
Memphis. Jackson was at the hospital the night of the murder, telling
reporters in the pandemonium that he had been the last man to talk
to King alive, that he had cradled King's shattered head in his arms.
Other King aides who had been on the balcony called Jackson a liar,
and one, Hosea Williams, physically attacked Jackson at the hospital.
All of this in the hours after the murder. Early the next morning,
April 5, 1968, Jesse Jackson turned up 500 miles north on NBC's
Today wearing a turtleneck shirt rust-red with what he claimed was

King's day-old blood. Jackson wore this shirt for something like 72 hours, doing two more talk shows in Chicago and attending a highly publicized memorial service for the slain civil rights leader.

The civil rights establishment, including King's widow, Atlanta Mayor Andrew Young, and now Atlanta City Councilman Hosea Williams, has never forgiven Jesse Jackson for the lie about the bloody turtleneck, if it was in fact a lie, which Jackson denies. Of King's old inner circle, only the late Ralph Abernathy, King's right arm since the Montgomery bus boycott, jailed and released with King in Albany, Georgia, on the day the 'well-dressed Negro' paid the fine, the man who by the testimony of Hosea Williams, Andrew Young, and others at the Lorraine Motel the evening of April 4, actually cradled King's head — only Ralph Abernathy was willing to endorse Jesse Jackson's 1988 presidential candidacy. The same eyewitnesses who name Abernathy as the man who held King place Jackson not on the balcony when King went down, but rather in the courtyard, waiting with the borrowed Cadillac hearse that was to transport King and his staff to a soul-food supper.

Time magazine's '87 election-season cover story on Jackson dwells on crime-scene details, *needing* to know whose blood it was, echoing unwittingly Warren Commission investigations of Oswald as lone gunman. Who was on the balcony of the Lorraine Motel that night? Who held King? If it wasn't King's blood on Jackson's turtleneck, whose blood was it? Did Jesse Jackson, in those 72 hours, April 4–6, 1968, actually go on nationwide television wearing a turtleneck spattered with, say, goat's blood? Or did he slash his forearm in the *Today* show's green room minutes before airtime, coming into 20 million guilty, scared, appalled households wearing his own blood?

Time claimed that it handled the turtleneck as a major news story because the incident reflected on the truthfulness of a presidential candidate. But if this was *Time*'s actual fascination, why give 3,000 words to the bloody turtleneck and a few sentences to the alleged mismanagement of HUD funds by Jackson's PUSH?

A deeper question: why does it matter whose blood it was? The turtleneck, even if splattered with King, was at most only a symbol of the horror on the balcony, just as the murder haunts our culture in part because it is itself a symbol of our blasted hope for peaceful change. Jackson's turtleneck, symbol of a symbolic killing, would be equally evocative if it only *looked* splattered. Since only our eyes experience the symbolic turtleneck, the shirt's 'true' even if stained with goat's blood, red paint, or menstruation. Isn't it?

No. Because deep symbols must partake of the actual. Just ask Aquinas: the Eucharist isn't as God, it *is* God. In the Mass and in the mass media.

The Martin Luther King Jr. Center for Nonviolent Social Change is Coretta Scott King's political base in Atlanta. The last four digits of its phone number, 1-9-5-6, commemorate the year of the Montgomery bus boycott that made the 26-year-old preacher a star. King's estate, of which widow King's Center is prime beneficiary, announced last year stepped-up efforts to stop widespread unlicensed use of Martin Luther King's face and voice, a vast rip-off nobody notices because King is somehow *expected* to be everywhere, on T-shirts, placards, coffee mugs, lunch boxes, posters, picture books, beach towels. Rappers probably owe the most royalties, since King makes many a sound-carpet cameo, but more is at stake here than revenue. 'Martin Luther King' is now a brand name, like 'Tylenol,' and uncontrolled use of King could be the strychnine in the painkiller. Much King-ing is vapid, thus harmless, like Michael Jackson's reliance on newsreel footage of the March on Washington to pad his "Man in the Mirror" video; or

U2's Bono, who orders crowds at concerts to sing along with King-tribute numbers 'in the name of the Reverend Martin Luther King'—Bono's probably OK so long as he doesn't try cashing traveler's checks in the name of Martin Luther King.

But other uses are potentially name-ruining, like poison aspirin. Ralph Abernathy's memoir of King included many juicy details of the slain civil rights leader's sex life, claiming that King had consummated no fewer than three sexual encounters before dusk on the day he stepped out onto the motel balcony. Abernathy is now an outcast among his old allies, though a suddenly wealthy author. Supporters of Lyndon LaRouche mounted a 'March on Washington' recently to protest the 'political' prosecution of their leader on charges ranging from extortion to tax evasion. Posters publicizing the March featured 2' × 3' photos of MLK, with text comparing King's civil disobedience to LaRouche's wire fraud. Conservative clergy seeking to make faith a force on the Republican Right in the mid-'70s took as conscious model King's Southern Christian Leadership Conference. Jerry Falwell, leader, spokesman, and media symbol of his cause, set out to be a white Martin Luther King. And Public Enemy's "Fight the Power" video features another re-enactment of the March on Washington, with King and moderate labor leader A. Philip Randolph replaced at the head of the column by Chuck D and Flavor Flav, who says Elvis was a racist and announces, formally, the failure of Reverend King's dream of bloodless integration. Widow King is probably not too enthusiastic about this use of the 'Martin Luther King' brand name, even less so in light of Jew-bashing quotes from P.E.'s 'Minister of Information' Professor Griff. Perhaps, in light of Griff's why-do-you-think-they-call-it-*jewelry?* statements, Public Enemy's March on Washington Square Park could do what J. Edgar Hoover's smears never did: give Martin Luther King—literally—a bad (brand) name. If the widow King waits, though, she will live to see Black Power rappers 'abused' just as Public Enemy 'abuses' her husband. If she's patient, she'll someday get to see Chuck D catch someone in court 'cause they stole *his* beat.

Rap's sonic chaos—the whir of culture in the blender—merely makes blatant something that has long been true: we struggle continually to tap our few truly compelling group symbols, always fearful that the symbol will be too potent to channel into the sane salesmanships of politics and entertainment. We fear the way the Beatles 'told' Charles Manson to murder. After all, you and Charles Manson both dream of oceans, but it's not the same Atlantic. Despite our ambivalence, the math of traffic in symbols goes on: there was 1 slain King, then 2 re-uses of King's symbol, and each re-use begets 2, so 4; then 8; 16: Bono, Chuck D, Schoolly D, Spike Lee, Michael Jackson, Jesse Jackson, Jerry Falwell, Lyndon LaRouche…

Widow King watched this begin during the first 'boosting' of her murdered husband that she couldn't stop, the *Today* show, April 5, 1968. She clearly never objected to the use of Martin Luther King; she merely wants to control the math, as if she owned not just the posthumous rights to the voice, but to every ear that heard it, and owned his four quarts and wherever they splattered, owned the turtleneck *and* the TVs. Her control is meant to be a way of mastering—*remastering*—grief.

But control is precisely what rap will not give her. Or me. Or you. Rappers don't pay the emotional royalties to the dead called grief, just as they refuse to pay one dime to James Brown, whose "Say It Loud (I'm Black and I'm Proud)" from '68 may be the real start of that wardrobe of 'tudes called rap. It is impossible to listen to more than 15 minutes of rap radio on any given night in Boston without

126

hearing a backbeat, a guitar hook, or a snatch of vocals from "Say It Loud." *Hours* of rap has found some part of itself in 4:46 of "Say It Loud." And James Brown, popularity waning in the late '70s, enjoys, as the backbone of Public Enemy's sound carpet, a huge new listenership. He's the uncredited (and, until the courts decide that sampling falls within federal copyright laws, uncompensated) father of a generation that thinks it's listening—and *is* listening—to original rap.

James Brown probably wouldn't recognize N.W.A as music. Certainly N.W.A is fundamentally alienated from the Georgia Bible-shouting that James Brown and Martin Luther King were raised on and that Brown later made into sweet, funky soul. Which is to say that James Brown would probably react to N.W.A approximately as Run-DMC first reacted to Aerosmith before they broke down the wall and saw the sea of ticket-buying Aerosmith fans. Or that James would react the way King, first black American to defy the law and briefly get away with it, would react to hearing N.W.A's '80s version of King's '60s defiance: Side 1, *Straight Outta Compton,* 51 violent acts bragged of, including 27 shootings, 9 stabbings, and 15 other assorted assaults. And of these 51 acts, only one—the execution of a cop—is violence against a white man. All the rest is black on black. It's the Old Testament King without the New Testament King. Like Jack Kemp's Kennedy: Martin Luther King as adjective, not noun.

N.W.A calmly replies that the brutality of their album isn't sensationalist: it's just the world they as ghetto teens call home. If *Straight Outta Compton* (or Schoolly D's *Smoke Some Kill* or Ice T's "Colors" or Public Enemy's "Sophisticated Bitch" or Q.B.C. or K-9 Posse or Just-Ice or any one of several hundred profit-turning rap records depicting violent acts) were mere symbol—imagined, fashioned, invented, dreamed of but not done—the work would admit the violent desires of the rappers and the fans who buy it.

Admitting violent fantasies is never chic both because of lingering Christian shame and because if the violence is merely imagined, this uncomfortably implies that the fantasizer isn't man enough to act it out. Doubly shamed: first, for wanting to; second, for not being able to.

N.W.A saves its audience from shame by being 'real.' Real beatings; real bitches; real blood. But even the most devout fan sneakingly suspects that rap's just another empty Hollywood, a special effect; that Schoolly D's literally all talk, more wrapper than rapper—a big, black, vinyl Eucharist to celebrate...what?

Rap is the bloody turtleneck.

D.
(3G)

THE OBVIOUS SOCIAL relevance of rap's new anti-themes, in terms of both urban black pathos and the integrity of white Social Order, raises those themes above the school-and-parents-are-a-drag straw man of rock's nascence and would seem to accord them a rough (if doubtless more 'marginal') musical equality with the largely white folk and rock rebellion-anthems of two decades past.[1]

Except in rap, as in rock, every against engages in miscegenation with a for. Realize that as a performer, besides the rhythmic

---

[1] Here's the big reason, sampling untalent and general mediocrity aside, why the spoiled, snarling Beastie Boys (the only exponents of white-teen 'hardcore' to achieve superstar status in crossover) are so godawful: they just have nothing imaginatively to hate or oppose except shrill old pop images of like the Mom who makes you go to school instead of lie around and get stoned, or some vague tight-ass 'oppression' that threatens your 'Right to Party.'

and prosodic constraints placed on him by hip-hop's substitution of rap and rhythm for tonal interplay as any cut's driveshaft, the rapper has an additional artistic challenge, one not faced by the stadium star conducted to and from his performance by chopper, or by the gnarled poet reciting for a seminar of weak-chinned supplicants ... or by those most daring of votaries, the pro-Right-to-Party P.A.C. of shriekers whose white audiences are secure in unity on the weight of a raised spiked fist alone. Viz., as before, the hip-hop artist must present himself and his rap to a tough audience as at once *for* and *of* that audience. He must hold in suspension both the projected artistic authority needed to get the attention of a young culture whose highest compliment is a terse 'I hear you,' *and* the witty pseudohumility required for the audience to validate his true defness, his historical and cultural in-the-Scene-ness as 'just a bad street nigga'[2] who 'used to rap in his basement'[3] before hitting it big; got 'his ass kicked'[4] daily just like the rest of the block's homeys; was, like them, trapped in 'madness, insanity ... profanity.'[5] For the audience, in other words, the rapper must literally be the homeboy next door ... except now a neighbor who's up on stage, rich and famous, via his *entitlement* to speak to, of, and for his community. This most vital and ubiquitous of personae, the just-like-you-only-more-so character, is variously well-served by an L.L. or Flav's swaggering gascon, by N.W.A's gangster-nihilist, by De La Soul's smiling parodies of white nitwits, by Schoolly D's near-Aesopian fox of a rapper. 'Both *of* and *for*' implies both the feckless wile of a

---

[2] N.W.A
[3] L.L. the Coolster
[4] Schoolly D
[5] Ice T

street kid and the hypnotic 'play' of one whose voice alone can carry a track or crowd. Now get ready, for the following is weird: The historical figures in whom these two crucial rapper identities best unite are, yes, the Blue Trickster of West African myth, but also the *actual* storytelling minstrel/troubadour of the European Dark Ages, the traveling rogue who performed for king and cooper both, singing (especially in Provençal) ever of himself. Recall that both the Trickster and the troubadour are limned in an antediluvian era long prior to the strange, deification-by-visibility of the modern pop 'star': the of-yore entertainer, like his audience, lived at a king or lord's fickle pleasure, or else survived in the forests by the very 'rapper's wit' his jokes and ballads extolled. In either case, integral to his validity was his unrecognizability — Blue Man never *looks* blue — his status as commoner, subject, one more person in and from the great rabble, one special Everyvoice that can, by organizing and instantiating a kind of libidinal sum of community parts, literally 'sing' to those special pavlovian places in listeners where abide true laughter, rage, celebration, lament.

It's the flip-flopped mix that's so riveting about the rap Scene's special elitist/Everyman aesthetic. Here you've got hundreds of thousands of $ worth of equipment devoted to manufacturing sounds whose birthright was the cheapness of the only available sound-making equipment; you've got 'manglers of technology' manipulating digital source codes like computer hackers; and all this behind the self-mocking mask of some itinerant musical character so old he's freaking pre-*European,* to say nothing of pre-Colonial. If the mainstream hype-currents flowed in the right direction, *this* is the kind of dizzying amillary-sphere of a new-music phenom that would be lauded as Out*rage*ous and In*geni*ous by the critics and P.R. engineers who can, these days, make such terms true the same way a minister can make you married—bare public pronouncement.

Instead it seems like the mainstream pop-critical bulk looks at, not through, the window's flawed bubbled glass, listens to a music-not-for-them just attentively enough to make out the blender-whining aural surface of a threatening Alien World—lyrics that sound shallow and materialistic instead of ingenious or inflaming; the self-obsessed boasts of the Soft rappers in Mets cap or silk suit; the intergroup musical snits between muscular, Ray-Banned Far-rakhanites who sound too often like unwitting parodies of come-dian E. Murphy's Angry Black Poet—'Kill Your Landlord!'[6]—the fixation on cars and jewelry, attractive ladies (always supine), biceps size, badness, guns... and good Lord how gauche *money*—why, many of the songs are to all appearances nothing but songs about getting paid for the songs!

If the formal constraints outlined throughout this sampler are what help limit and define the rap genre's possibilities, it's usually 'content' issues—the musical mugging of classic precursors, or the wearying self-consciousness of the rap itself—that best alienate mainstreams, help keep this riparian genre so insulated, dammed, not-for-, fresh. A serious, black-directed rap's successful crossover to a truly national, multiracial record public won't be possible unless the largely white, conservative worlds of record distribution, promotion, and criticism can find some way to reach an accommo-

---

[6] See for instance black intellectual critic Stanley Crouch: 'There is far too much proof that racism is no more the invention of white people than white people were, as Malcolm X taught so many while under the thrall of "Elijah Muhammed," invented by a mad black scientist'... in an '89 *NR* piece about what he calls the 'Afro-Fascist Chic' of Public Enemy, Spike Lee, 2 Live Crew, etc.

dation with stories that don't play by Our rules, seem either horribly Ugly and Mean and Depressing, or else (maybe worse) so darn Self-Conscious and Swaggering and well just *Vulgar*. . . . Not at all like the good, charming, *safe* black music we've been taught to digest. Just imagine. The idea of, say, Lionel Richie singing, not about lost love, but about his own singing about lost love, about his own incomparable talent at really singing about singing about lost love. Imagine Lionel Richie singing an attack on the dicklessness of a Michael Jackson or a Roland Gift. Imagine Lionel Richie singing about some radio network's wimpy, shortsighted neglect of his work. All this would be bad enough, empty and circular: odes to the ode itself. But now try to image good old reliable Lionel somehow singing about how much booty, bootey, acclaim, and prestige rightly accrue to himself and his song: some sort of all-new ode to the ode's own *fair market value*. . . well pardonnez-moi but this'd just seem beyond the literal pale of what's art, what has any right to be popular, what's even worth ear time, much less entertainment dollar. No?

Probably no, is the thing. . . though the following may very well seem obnoxious or opinionated. It seems like there has long been some diathetic Puritan reticence in white people that makes Us uncomfortable with any open mention of people's salaries, assets, the prices or value of Our *things*.[7] In my parents' time it was just regarded as vulgar, a verbal scratch of the crotch. It's only under the last ten years of political helmsmanship that younger U.S. whites have begun to regard open, wet-mouthed acquisitiveness as

---

[7] Where I grew up most people were farmers, and the phenomenon was called 'talking poor'; but the general neurosis seems to intensify in direct relation to one's income and education.

fashionable, to see consumption as value and not just value's crude measure, to speak openly about American Dream as financial fantasy... especially to do so with irony, where the late-'80s eye-roll and elbow-nudge can keep a screen of self-mockery between Us and any genuine expression of self that could make anybody uneasy. . . .

No psychosociologists on staff, here, but it seems fair to posit that the odd little anal hang-ups of an ethnic majority need not be shared even by those minority Others who share its space and borders. Marginal communities, living out their own enforced phylogeny of deprivation and insecurity, forced by exclusion, crowding, and historical function in on themselves to locate shared value or model, seeing as op-/apposite their grinding poverty and dependence on bureaucracies only the contrasts of 2-D *Dynasty* image, superrich athletes and performers, and the drug and crime executives for whom visible affluence is part of the job description — such a culture in such a place and time might well be excused[8] for equating success and accomplishment directly with income, display, prestige. The very funniest raps (L.L.'s "Jack the Ripper," P.E.'s "Son of Public Enemy (Flavor-Whop Version)," Eric B. & Rakim's "Paid in Full") parody their and their own set's fixation on money — not 'wealth' or 'security' but bucks, dead prez's, greenbacks, moneymoneymoney — as well as the national environment in which such shallow,[9] dubiously tasteful obsessions can rise with sufficient public force to yield an Art's theme and subject, context, even 'value.'

---

[8] Granted, the quintessential outsider's term.

[9] Don't for one moment think the rappers don't know it's shallow: it's part of the '80s loop they've mastered.

In the obsessions themselves we might be able to see the outer limits of a famed 'openness' within marginal communities about subjects and issues — e.g., sexuality, drugs, religion, self-esteem, ecstatic joy, deep loss, etc. — that the white U.S. mainstream has almost had to be trained to hear about without blushing or wrinkling aquilines or carrying pickets — a 'lack of inhibition'[10] that helps explain why a comparatively tiny and deprived subnation exerts such a disproportionate influence on American popular music that it can be said to have invented it. For the best of that pop, whether folk or jazz or Blues or the rock 'n' roll that was all rebellion, is always first and last ABOUT FREEDOM — where 'about' connotes both 'to speak of' and 'to work toward' and where 'freedom' means freedom from the muting cingula of circumstances, forces, *norms*. For early rock, these norms were most often generational, the forces ideological — a prison of the mind that the Young Democrat or teen heard, finally *felt* in the music was escapable . . . simply because the music *was* the escape. One could, in certain halcyon Demand Side days, effect change by singing of change (Dr. King), escape what one disliked via musics or the lifestyles behind them (psychedelics, hippies, Dead-Heads), trust pop music to be *of* what it was *about*.

And so in many ways — yes, several of them perverse — you can see rap pushing the formal and thematic freedom-envelope back at a rate not seen since the days of Dean and Presley. Freedom

---

[10] Again, the only thing that can save our asses credibility-wise is an open admission that these terms are, must be, the noises that inevitably accompany *any* cross-cultural observations with even the barest hint of 'norm' to them. But we depend heavily on such an admission's corollary: as long as the relativism is kept brightly in mind, the observations aren't necessarily w/o some value.

has been declared from the melodics-harmonics formulae of composition, from the careful demographics of the Catchy Tune. 'Motherfucker,' 'cocksucker,' etc. now raise eyebrows on hardly anyone but radio programmers. Verbal restraints imposed by even the slightest post-'70s sensitivity to differences of sex and inclination are trampled. Most, the idea that a popular music is primarily an entertainment, chewing gum for the eustachian, a something-happy-to-take-people's-minds-off-____, with no affirming last verse or shaggy-dog punch line or *vision*—or at least no oppressive garble of sample carpet designed to make people too claustrophobic even to move to the danceable backbeat—this noble, time- and capital-tested idea has been tossed out a closed window...and all in the name of the hoary aesthetic principle of *mimesis!* Plato lives, downtown! The world depicted in rap is short&nasty&brutish precisely because the world sung of is the one sung for....And the urban-'80s world sung for is a troubled, undersupplied, drug- and crime-riddled lacuna in the American text, one to which the most oppressive raps are just corrigenda. It's a rude place—people say 'motherfucker' and 'cocksucker' in lieu of 'kiddo' and 'big fella.' The literal lyric reference to weapons and crack and cock is, for neither better nor worse, the reference the rapper's world 'relates to,' the imaginative space it abides, the arena in which the freedom all pop extols exercises its play.

...Is it real freedom, though: a world where Chuck D can serenade his Uzi in art exactly *because* in the S. Bronx 'Uzi's' such a perfect metonym for irresistible force? For all the exciting formal innovations and transformations of rap, what's finally, for us, its most affecting quality is that it's the first pop genre to countenance a peculiarly modern American despair, one for which popular music, maybe any popular art, can no longer be a palliative—all

136

the putative 'freedoms' such art invents and exploits and rips off and wastes finally resembling most closely, today, the prisoner's COMPLETE FREEDOM to beat his head on the cell wall just as much as he likes. Serious rap's the first music to begin creative work on the new, (post-) postmodern face the threat of economic inequality to American ideals is wearing: the dreadfully obvious one: viz., 'freedom' becomes not qualitative but quantitative, quantifiable, a cold logical function of where you are and what you have to exercise it on. For the unfree citizen, U.S. freedom now equals the very 'power' it invented itself against. Little wonder that in rap the constitutional watchwords of white public discourse detach, emptify, float: oh Jesus *surely* freedom can't be just the wherewithal to buy and display. If it is, then the whole country's been lied to by itself, and if the impending millennium turns out Millennial it'll be hard to fucking care. But if true freedom's still meant to be more than this, more than the Pursuit of Yuppiness, then these are some really pathetic, infuriating times—especially among the Marginal, on whom freedom's unjust absence has imposed the conviction that freedom's just presents.

D.
(3H)

SITTING THERE AND listening to the canon's repetition over and over until you start to feel the blank understanding that is perhaps the purview of the outsider alone is pretty much the only way to subscend rap's yes vulgar Alien surface and hear this pathos, the sort of true-music quality best felt on the ungrooved silences between tracks, the places where the listener gets to breathe;...the best way to see that most mainstreamers' 'self-reference' objections to rap don't miss the point so much as simply aim off target—point, by custom, toward here, the 'free' world, the corporate-pop target, mint-white but for a tiny dark central dot.

Yes it's *true:* L.L. Cool J's big hit "I'm That Type of Guy" is a self-love song, ostensibly sung to 'You,' the man L.L.'s cuckolding. Grimace grimace. So an L.L. Cool J sings too much of a Himself he makes too much of? Simple answer: he's saying he exists. The Soft rap's the postmodern love song. The love song's traditional fixation on the Other—charms of, quest for, union with, loss of—has long been acknowledged as token for a more basic human urge toward some kind of completion, a fulfillment-in-being that we intuit's been damaged or lost. The Fall, Plato's leaky sieve, T. S. Eliot's Arthurian infertility, etc., on and on: Quest, *Romance*. In terms of deprivation, the traditional love-singer is both lucky and un-: feeling, with an intensity we don't have to, just how incomplete he really is; but at the same time getting to *believe*, as we rarely can, that he's figured out what's missing, and has only to acquire the love object for her/it to become for him *tessera*, the fixative that'll let him be, glue him together, whole. That his belief in completion-via-object is ultimately stupid we never have to hear about in the love songs themselves, since quests *ex officio* end with Acquisition or Honeymoon at the very outside. But the postmodern love song, the Soft rap, alters the equation, and turns the desperation up a notch: it's the rapper's *own* defness, his *face*, his own projected *image* that he needs, thus loves. And the (post-) postmodern terror attendant on even *imagining* his image's absence will not permit the rapper one second's vision of that absence, won't let him yearn musically for its presence or mourn its loss: the def image, the face, must continually be extolled, celebrated, kept 'fresh' in order to stay on at all.

And is it a surprise that face, defness, and image in this community, able still to afford only to watch and listen, are largely a matter of TV virtues—physical courage, strength, viciousness, appeal for the opposite sex, plus the visibles: fashions, precious baubles, weaponry, wheels? Here too it's just clearly no fair of Us to berate artists for buying into the values their community and context supply. But *nor* is it fair, as even the broadest-minded Big Critics are wont, simply to shift the indictment from aesthetic to social and from artist to audience, to decry the 'naive materialism' that seems to inform so large a part of the young black community as evidence of any moral vacuity or pre-American atavism.[1]

Basically it's not fair because there's a real and marvelously unmeant beauty to the rap Scene's materialism, today. In no other music for no other audience can we see the Supply Side Republican vision of America's '80s so carefully decocted, rendered, *loved*. We're talking here less about wattle-jowled speeches on the need to get Big Government off backs that are marching stolidly into an affluent dreampast than we are about those speeches' and that somnambulistic march's inevitable trickle-down — the way, as 'average' American incomes soared and business revved on behind-the-scenes yen, the same popular electronic landscapes the rappers have mined in their effort to mirror a here-and-now began pulsing with the signals of a whole new yuppoid aesthetic, an attitude we all[2] pretended was cultured, so-very-phisticated, so here-and-now. Anyone can see these signals' lights, at night. Can hear them in any ungrooved black wax. Listen. Greed is good. Power is good. Power is freedom. Power is determined by the credibility of your threats. Power is quantitative and measurable via how others regard you. Power is possessing an image of strength and resolution sufficient to force credulity and regard on others. The exercise of power — overspending, violence, selfishness, disdain for truth or feeling — these are acceptable means of attaining ends a powerful nation or person really needs and deserves. What individuals really need and

---

[1] Cf., again, that sternest of fathers, Crouch: 'Cowardice, opportunism, and the itch for riches by almost any means necessary define the demons within the black community. The demons are symbolized, among others…by Afro-fascist race-baiters like Public Enemy.'

[2] This is one thing rap misses: why paranoia's still insane, today: there doesn't have to be a conspiracy if we all think alike.

deserve most is the money to buy the things that determine their 'class,' aka their 'face,' aka their freedom, aka their power, aka the degree of credulity and regard bestowed on them by one huge marching column that All Thinks Alike. Because cars, hardware, jewelry, trendy clothes, are the uniforms of those who exist on the electronic landscape to be regarded at all. And *you too* must 'Have It All,' must 'Succeed, Not Just Survive.'[3]

To sum up Now, then: to be, you must be able to buy; to be credible, you must in fact buy; but to be def, fresh, *regarded*—to be not just the object of statistics and abstractions and advertants but yourself the object of a Lover's/Enemy's/Community's/Nation's great big ontologizing Stare—to be Enfaced, you must have, buy, and *display*.

The beauty is the way all this stuff is stripped to its glowing bones in a Marginal music without any of the old puritanic baggage about public verbal Taste that in the white community breeds a near-slapstick hypocrisy, one whereby most of us loudly ridicule an '80s 'consumerism that borders on the onanistic' while composing high-Nielsen audiences for *Lifestyles, Dallas,* so on. It could well be that, conceived in rural, shit-kicking Illinois, then born in Beverly Hills, real Reaganism just wasn't ever designed for segments of the population who tend to let what they've bought all hang out.

Not that the Marginal have bought it *all,* and this too makes the rap Scene a neat, scary place to observe economics, art & politics try to work themselves out. The rapper's world is one that seems to embrace completely the Reagan carrots of Entitlement and Power, a deregulated *prenez-faire* where freedom is isomorphic with class, and face is a stat-function of one's capital and consumption. Some mild peculiarities of the urban black '80s experience, though, complicate

---

[3] Ads: beer and financial services, respectively.

and compromise the embrace. In no communities like the urban and Marginal has the great-sounding conservative promise of surgery on Big Government been kept so well or revealed so thoroughly as nothing more than the strategic ablation of unprofitable social sectors: cuts in Medicaid, in scheduled welfare and Social Security increases, in funding for HUD, for job and job-training programs, for health- and day-care, sanitation, recreation, literacy, and feasible-alternatives-to-drugs programs have had the long-known but little-mentioned consequence that the actual quality of life in poor urban communities declined further just while all around them, in the manicured neighborhoods west and north—plus of course dead ahead, in the cathode's glass—lifestyles of luxury, freedom, power, consumption, and display seemed now so firmly in place, so right, they were actually being whitely *flaunted.*

Yr. staff posits that the rapper's is a Scene that has accepted—yea, *reveres*—the up-to-date values and symbols of a Supply Side prosperity, while rejecting, with a scorn not hard to fathom, what seem to remain the 'rules' for how the Marginal are supposed to improve their lot therein: viz., by studying hard, denying themselves, working hard, being patient, keeping that upper lip stiff in the face of what look like retractions of the last 'great society's' promises to them, denying themselves, working hard and slowly at the restricted number and salary of jobs available in/to their community; waiting, *patiently,* for the lucre of billion-dollar corporate tax breaks and Wall Street monte to trickle their way. We posit that, for serious rap, these Protestant patience- and work-ethic rules, the *really* nostalgia-crazed parts of Supply Side, just don't reconcile with the carrots, the enforced and reinforced images of worth-now as wealth-now, of freedom as just power, of power as just the inclination and firepower to get what you decide you have coming to you. The Real American Way, no? ... Entitlement has always had a two-word response for Impediment.

If all this is so, the bourgeois-less economics of the '89 ghetto are easy to explain. Poverty is all you see around, and then there's nauseous wealth straight ahead, behind convex glass, in Stereo Where Available. The best rappers both exemplify and ridicule the contradictions inherent in '80s conservatism, in mixed images of political democracy and economic Hobbesianism. In rap we have the Voice of a community of whom it's just plain unreasonable to expect trust in white Systems, but for whom the rewards of the System's stress on image, power, status, and greed are broadcast too frequently and too forcefully to be unreal. What would *you* do, or sing about?

Another pretty simple answer, from outside the window: even the best of rap has no 'vision' of anything beyond present discontent less because it's a black music than because it's a distinctively *young* one. Ours is a generation (late- or post-Boom) divorced from Time: we're taught to look to the 'innocent past' for signposts to value; to see the present as little more than a compendium of evils and past fuckups we have to borrow a couple trillion from the Japanese and throw an innocent-past party to forget; to see the future as a vague fairyland where the consequences of our dire present will by political wand-waving 'all work out,' or else as the grim, cinereous end-of-the-month day when the Visa charges we've been using to pay off our AmEx finally come due. And the time banditry has got to be specifically worse for the urban black young, since the only real 'past' that might summon *its* political pavlovs is that of a civil rights movement no one under 30 can recall, of a King and an X both murdered at rhetorical zenith, before the movements their words fashioned had barely begun transit. Because the past can be considered altered, falsified (for whites by Reagan, for blacks by the whites who ran the past), induction doesn't apply, and so no imaginative future can exist: at best it'll be more of the same. Today even the *fresh*est black music is no longer an 'escape' from the very conditions and tight borders that make it possible as music, or even as expression—since rap is, in the best and worst ways, just a mirror.

M., God love him, limits his best point to sitcoms. In fact rap is 'weird' the way only an art invented by people born post-'50s can be weird: it's Timeless: there is for it only a limitless, unframed *here-and-now,* a contextless buzzing *Scene,* from inside. Rap's special def genius is its near-Digital loop: it's turned its Scene's horror—its betrayal by history, its bombardment by contradictory signal, its violent impotence, its insularity and claustrophobia and absence of egress—turned a Scene's precise horror into precise, cutting-edge art. You lose consolation, but you gain a new kind of jagged, unforgiving mimesis—Plato sampled while on the john.

Serious rap's so painfully real because it's utterly mastered the special '80s move, the 'postmodern' inversion that's so much sadder and deeper than just self-reference: rap resolves its own contradictions by *genuflecting* to them. See how. The intensity of Fad but the life span of Genre? Rap's here-and-now is always *here-and-now:* a music without a future tense can't but be immortal. A music that screams, with Schoolly D, 'No more fuckin Rock 'n' Roll!' can't but be a vital force on rock. A music that collapses the distinction between homage and infringement, signal and rule—shit, Self and Other—in the rip-off that is sampling can't but be 'original' in how it plunders and mangles and re-uses; for a signal without rules is also without precedent, just as 'stealing' means nothing when nothing can be owned. A music less 'against' than simply scornful of the cold blank caucasian System of special hypocrisies can't but be of compelling interest to those white of us who stand all scrubbed

and eager at that magnifying impediment of glass that rappers —
like all U.S. young — have built themselves into. It may be, as
avant-avant-gardists were arguing, gee, only 70 or 80 years back,
that 'self-reference' itself is like anything that defines a genre, a
Scene, a place-and-time — just another window, thick and unclean,
bulletproof and parallax, where where you stand informs what you
look at, where sound and gesture split and everything Outside's
quiet and everyone's alone, and free.

M.

(31)

WE CARE

is what the banner over the parking lot of the Roxbury Community
College says, and it doesn't take genius to deduce that the WE is
black parents and their children and what they CARE about is saving their own and loved ones' lives from the gangbanging that's
rocking Roxbury. The banner alone doesn't tell you this, of course,
and were it hung at an auto show, you'd be entitled to conclude that
the WE meant Edsel collectors and CARE meant car care. But look
around: this is not an auto show.

A bad but good-intentioned local rap act called Young Nation
is on stage and a few hundred kids shake butt. Earlier, two toddlers
lip-synched Roxbury native Bobby Brown's "Don't Be Cruel"; later
city councilors and prominent preachers will orate. Two teens have
painted half their faces white, in an effort (you overhear them
telling a *Boston Globe* stringer) to 'break the color barrier.'

It's been a summer of murder and rallies. Boston's gangs have been at war over slights and sales territories since the last peacekeeping Boss, a kind of homeboy Roman Emperor, was assassinated. His name was Tony C. Johnson, and he's been interred at Roxbury's Mount Hope cemetery since June '87. But things took a turn for the ugly during Christmas week of '88, when somebody killed a silhouette they thought was Mervin Reese, leader of the Humboldts. The silhouette was in fact Reese's 41-year-old machinist stepdad. Reese survived; the reputed triggerman, who was found slumped over the wheel of a stolen car the next day, did not. A Suffolk County grand jury said that Reese later put two bullets into a kid named Romero Holliday, boss of the rival Castlegate gang. Holliday retaliated by shooting wildly at a group of Reese's followers idling on a street corner, while pedaling past on his bicycle.

Yet another slug intended for a Humboldt hit the base of a streetlight and ricocheted into the head of an 11-year-old girl named Darlene Tiffany Moore. She wasn't the first bystander hit in the gang war, nor even the first that week, but something about the ricochet electrified Roxbury. Tiffany Moore became another Linda Brown (of *Brown v. Board*), another black child serving as popular symbol of What's Wrong. An emotional rally was held at which the gangs and the Boston Police Department were both booed, and the group called WE CARE was formed. Several other demonstrations followed, including a rally led by Jesse Jackson that was itself controversial. The march was routed far away from black neighborhoods for fear of scaring off whites who might otherwise join in. Some community organizers felt that a protest against gangs and crack in the heart of the pricey Back Bay shopping district sent at best a mixed message. Many whites thought that if it was safe to march in Roxbury, they wouldn't need to. A day later, a computer programmer, who had trundled his children to the march because he wanted them to be able to say they had seen Jesse Jackson, was pulled from his car by gang members and murdered at a stoplight in Dorchester.

You are not here because you are among the WE who CARE, although you do. You are writing about rap and looking for Gary Smith, co-owner of RJam Productions, a local label dabbling in rap. You had heard a rumor that Tam-Tam, Gary's prize prospect rapper, had been signed by Arista, a deal in the negotiation stage when you last talked to Gary. A breakthrough, if true.

You spy some kids you once saw hanging out at RJam's studios. They're probably in the eighth grade. Prime gang recruits: old enough to be responsible with the kinds of $ drug couriers handle, not old enough to be tried as adult offenders. With this caring thought in your head, you walk up to them. 'Hey,' you say, 'you guys seen Gary Smith around?'

The kids look at you funny and sort of filter off into the crowd. You realize that you must look and sound exactly like a cop. What do you say to convince somebody that you're no more a cop than they are?

※

Heard on the FM as we argued about this essay's ending: Public Enemy, perhaps the four most dangerous men in America (and maybe our best rappers), were breaking up; or, more accurately, were not getting back together as a foursome after their July '89 breakup, since this is the third or fourth rumored-non-reunion-after-rumored-reunion, all fallout from the mushroom cloud of media attention that followed Professor Griff's recommendation that a *Washington Times* reporter heed the Jew-bashing writings of automaker Henry Ford. Still mere rumor as of this writing. The Griff Business exploded in July '89. The Woman of that fateful month, *Playboy*'s Miss July, listed among her favorite 'musicians' both Aerosmith, with whom Run-DMC found bliss on "Walk This Way," and L.A. rapper Ice T, who plays no musical instruments. A sure sign of rap's arrival: even Our pinups are listening.

The moral: hurry. Rap's offer's good for a limited time only. Its Bachs are as fleeting as Miss Julys. Pithy bit here about an art that trashes its past having no future. But Public Enemy would surely cut the same deal all over again: freedom to reinvent funk, to make dance music of Dr. King and of dentists' drills, to say what they think even when they haven't thought it through, all at the price of the life span of a pinup or gangbanger. Because fuck Abe Lincoln: Griff's all about living free — both in the sense that his posse paid no royalties *and* in the sense that sampling springs the rapper from the jail of being limited only to the sounds the rapper can, by himself, make. Which freedom P.E. in their prime used to scream how little control anybody had over them.

Rappers are Miltonic devils:

> *My life on earth*
> *Was hell, my friend.*
> *And when I die,*
> *Going to hell again*

vows whoever cut a rap I heard once in June '89 over WILD-AM/Boston and have never since been able either to trace or forget. 'I worked like a slave to become a master,' another rapper boasts. And 'master' means both the studio-produced tape FedExed by the big corporation to its record-pressing plant (as in: *I worked like a slave to become a slick digitally altered product that may not sound like me live) and* the remembered slave owner (as in: *I worked like a slave and now I own them*). Rappers, like the Elizabethans, love reversals. To 'serve' means what it meant in Nat Turner's time, but also to deflower. It means both to work under and to work over.

There are deeper reversals afoot. The Stop the Violence Movement, founded in '88, is a kind of "We Are the World" for rappers; except that the 'We' is *We young blacks* and 'the World' is *Anyplace where joining a gang is tempting,* since the Stop the Violence EP, "Self Destruction," is one long plea from 14 of hip-hop's bigger names to bag out of gangs. The tone is lofty. Tens of millions of $ of rap talent chant, almost as if rooting for it, 'SELF-DESTRUCTION YOU'RE HEADED FOR SELF-DESTRUCTION.' Kool Moe Dee scolds while teaching history:

> *Back in the sixties our brothers & sisters were hanged*
> *How could you gangbang?*
> *I never ever ran from the Ku Klux Klan*
> *I shouldn't have to run from a black man.*

Troublingly, most of the Stop the Violence 14 made their names signifying violence, including Just-Ice (the self-proclaimed "Gangster of Hip-Hop"), Chuck "My Uzi Weighs a Ton" D, and KRS-One, who posed on the cover of his first LP brandishing what looks from where I sit like an MAC-10 semi-automatic pistol. Chuck D would argue that his pre–Stop the Violence use of killing as metaphor for excelling was a case of talking to ghetto kids in a language they get. And he has a point. One reason why the "We Are the World" crew failed to move us—or move *anything,* except records at Christmastime—is that their *We* and their *World* were not earned. What business has cheekboned millionaire Californian Harry Belafonte including, say, a Boston Irish lawyer in his *We* or his *World?* His was a showbiz *We,* a big Sammy Davis Junior talk-show hug, arms around everything that is.

Stop the Violence was, if nothing else, medicine against the many fake, unearned *We*s killing the U.S., from "We Are the World" to the Pepsi Generation to the Live Studio Audience to Nixon's Silent Majority. 'We urge to merge,' Chuck D and Flavor Flav duet to close Stop the Violence's rapped ad against gangs:

CHUCK & FLAV: We live for the love of our people the hope.

CHUCK: They get along.

CHUCK & FLAV: Yeh! So we did a song.

CHUCK: Gettin' the point to our brothers and sisters who don't know the time.

FLAV: Boyee! So we wrote a rhyme.

CHUCK: It's dead in your head, you know, I'll drive to build and collect ourselves with intellect.

FLAV: Come on.

CHUCK: To revolve, to evolve to self-respect.

CHUCK & FLAV: 'Cause we got to keep ourselves in check or else

CHUCK: It's...

EVERYBODY: SELF-DESTRUCTION YOU'RE HEADED FOR SELF-DESTRUCTION.

REPEAT.

MC/DFW
Summer '89

PERMISSIONS ACKNOWLEDGMENTS

ACKNOWLEDGMENTS

I, I'm, me, and *mine* are spoken several hundred times on N.W.A's *Straight Outta Compton,* an album-length brag from '88. But the vinyl's sold in a cardboard sleeve crowded with fine-print thank-yous, acknowledging all that *I, I'm, me,* and *mine* owe cops, rappers, God, the Dodgers, and 256 named others. Def—*and* debt—be not proud.

We, too, owe. Schoolly D, Public Enemy, De La Soul, and many others brought the noise without which our experiment in listening would've been damn difficult. Lee Smith, formerly of The Ecco Press, now of Atheneum, is more responsible than any other single human for this ms. seeing daylight as a book.

Some shared insights from their lives in hip-hop, particularly Gary Smith, Reese Thomas, Ralph Stacey, and the girl rapper Tam-Tam of Boston's RJam Productions. Others lent comfort and cold showers at various stages, including Daniel Halpern and Lee Ann Chearneyi of The Ecco Press, Lisa Cortes of Polygram, Bonnie Nadell of Frederick Hill Associates, Richard Smith, Mdiawar Abim-bole, Phillip "DJ Plate Lunch" Jackson, Brad Moltz, Ann Patchett, Colette de Labry, J. C. Foulsham, Ian "MC Mixed Results" Penny, and the indulgent folks at Ocean Records, Roxbury, MA.

Thanks to everyone. The merits of this book are substantially yours; the flaws are entirely my coauthor's.

Pax
MC/DFW
Boston
Oct '89